SHORT STORIES

THE AUTOBIOGRAPHY OF COLUMBUS SHORT

COLUMBUS SHORT

With
MARISA MENDEZ

1

THE ROAD TO NOWHERE

I'm standing on the 101 with a bottle of chardonnay in my hand, dressed in $6,000 worth of clothing that I didn't even own. I walked straight off the set of *Scandal* in full wardrobe, after I checked my pocket and made sure I had my credit card and my I.D. For some reason, I had my passport on me too, and that was all I needed to get a car to the airport and just never come back.

The screw-off bottle of chardonnay I was sipping as I walked toward the freeway came from that liquor store next to Roscoe's on Gower. It was right there as I walked off the lot. You're not allowed to drink liquor openly in Los Angeles, but that was someone else's problem to deal with. My world was spinning, and I didn't know much, but I knew I was about to disappear. I didn't want this anymore. I couldn't do it for another day. I was ready to check out. I didn't want to die in that moment, but I wanted this part of me to die. The part that felt anything.

Deep in thought

February 12, 2012 was the date, and I'll never forget it. 2/12/12. I wasn't an expert on numerology, but this was something that I just couldn't ignore. Somebody was trying to tell me something. It was episode 212 of *Scandal* that we were shooting that day. Ironically, 12 symbolizes God's power and authority in the Bible, so I read this as

God trying to take control of the shit pile my home life had become.

But let me back up a little.

My then-best friend wanted to come see me at work that day, and my then-wife — her name isn't relevant so we'll call her *that girl* — did too. They both had visitor passes set up for them, and just before we wrapped for lunch, the Assistant Director told me my wife was on set. Cool, I'll be done in about 30 minutes and I'll go to her. I'd already told my boy Ronnie to let me know when my wife arrived, but for whatever reason, he doesn't tell me until 45 minutes later that she'd "just" pulled up on the lot. I thought that was weird, but maybe he didn't see her earlier. Whatever, it's not that serious.

I go to meet up with *that girl* and I see my best friend coming out of the parking garage, tucking his pants in and getting himself together. I hadn't really had enough time to formulate an actual thought about it, because no sooner than I saw him, I see the ADs approaching me. They hover around me and lead me away, as someone is telling them to put me in the office. I don't know who called them, I don't even know why they called them. I don't know why I'm being escorted away. I literally just don't even have a thought in my head at this point, because I'm more focused on why everyone is staring at me as the ADs are guiding me off the set. It felt like I was in high school again and I was being sent to the principal's office. Close enough. As I enter the big office and the ADs close the door behind me, there sitting are Shonda Rhimes, one of the *Scandal* producers Merri Howard and one of the executive producers, Betsy Beers. They're looking at me so seriously, and I can hear my heart start beating in my ears.

"What's going on guys?"

Shonda shook her head and looked me in the eyes.

"Columbus, your life is a hot ass mess," she says in a tone of partial sympathy and full authority.

She wasn't lying. I'd always been ashamed of my life, and though I wasn't necessarily "hiding" it, I never opened up to anyone on set, let alone the world...because if they knew the half, I felt like everyone would judge me. Now I was facing the jury.

At this point, I still don't actually know what I'm about to be hit with. I'm thinking that Shonda had somehow become privy to the issues my wife and I were going through at home, so I start to tell her that it's okay and that my wife and I would get through it. I was a little off, though.

"Your wife is fucking your best friend, Columbus! Wake up!"

That's exactly how she hit me with it — straight, no chaser. You know how in cartoons when they get hit over the head and all of those stars appear as their eyes roll around? That's exactly how I felt. The acme anvil had indeed crushed me into a pancake. Only it wasn't funny! The floor fell out from under me, I couldn't hear anything anymore, I couldn't think. All I remember is getting up as they were talking. Their voices were coming through like the adults on Charlie Brown, where you don't make out what they're saying, just a bunch of "wah wah wah" sounds with no descript annunciation of anything. I can't hear them, but I can see my feet moving. I just started walking.

I walked out of the office, got on the elevator and continued off the lot across the street to a liquor store. And I just didn't stop. I kept going down Sunset toward the 101 in my $3500 John Paul Smith suit and my Gucci tie, and I had no plans to look back.

Darby Stanchfield and I

As I approached the freeway, a white van pulled up alongside me. When the sliding door opened, I saw Kerry Washington, Darby Stanchfield and Katie Lowes all looking at me with tears in their eyes, telling me to get in the car. To see those faces and hear them tell me that and knowing all that was going on, it was so much. And you know, you can tell someone to get in the car, but if they're not ready to get in the car... if they're not ready to break these curses out here, there's nothing you can do at that point.

That day was truly one of the worst days of my life. That feeling, that pit inside my stomach—it's a feeling I can't ever forget. And here I am dealing with this and I wasn't even on drugs at the moment. I was the moral leader for my team and I dropped the ball still, because I couldn't let this toxic relationship go. I was more comfortable in toxicity than I could ever be with peace.

Peace made me uncomfortable. I liken it to a stray dog I met in Puerto Rico while filming. One of my co-stars ended up taking in the dog we found running around base camp, starved and homeless in the middle of the jungle.

That co-star took the dog home that night and got it a warm new doggy bed and placed it by the fireplace with a nice treat. But oddly, I was told, the dog grabbed the treat and ran outside on the patio and laid down in the pouring rain enjoying it with no care of the torrential downpour coming down on him. He was so used to being in the jungle with no bed, no fire, no cover. He felt at home in the storm! That dog was me!

How do you show up for a show when your real life could compete with the script? If I wasn't already fired, I wanted to quit — and if it wasn't for Kerry, I would have.

Kerry Washington and I at the NAACP Awards

"Just finish this season out, Columbus! Don't quit the show!" Kerry told me that day. "We're all here for YOU."

"For me? How? This is your show."

"No, we're all here for you. You don't get it. You're not getting it. I need you to have my back. Just stay here until we finish the season and then we can decide what you want to do after that."

So, I did. Even though I wanted to pull a Dave Chappelle and just vanish, I had to get back to work. In hindsight, that was probably the best thing for me that day. Who knows where I'd be if they didn't come get me? They got me a hotel that night to make sure I was safe, and the next day I went to work without incident. I wish I could say that was the end of my chapter with my wife, though.

When she called me the next day, I had already put together all the pieces. I wanted to see my daughter, though, and I still wanted to hear my wife's side of the story—against my better judgment. I didn't want to break up a family or the system that we had in place, you know? My life had order, as dysfunctional as it was. Of course, I wasn't okay with it, but I found my okay at the bottom of the bottle.

At the end of the season, Shonda told me that she wanted me to go to rehab.

"I know you don't necessarily need to go, but based on everything that's happened in the last month, the network is saying either you go or you definitely don't have a job next season."

"Honestly, I was thinking... Shonda, I don't know if I want a job next season."

"Columbus, listen to me. Go to rehab and get yourself together and come back. We're going to be here. We're going to love you and support you. We're your family."

And so I went. My time in rehab was amazing honestly. I was reluctant in going and apprehensive (to say the least) to be with people I thought were in way worse condition than I was. However, in the end it was one of the best experiences of my life. I was truly beginning to understand the core of my substance abuse. The real why's! After thirty days of extensive therapy, group sessions and in-depth character analysis, I felt I was ready to return to my life. The whole cast wrote me this great letter while I was there and sent it to me before I got out, which was just before we started rehearsals. I was welcomed back to the *Scandal* set with open arms and love and grace and passion and non-judgement and it was wonderful.

I did have a family. They all delivered on that promise. I'm eternally grateful for that because without them, it could have been exponentially worse. But what I failed to realize was that just because I did the work and I began to change, that doesn't mean the world I lived in changed along with me.

When I got with my now ex-wife, I was just so in love...or lust! For once in my life, I felt like I was going to finally have peace! I'm going to make a family! It's funny because I used to tell my mom, "It can't be this difficult to be married! Why do you keep getting married? It can't be this hard! You keep introducing men to us and then they're gone and this is why I don't want to get my hopes up anymore!" Man, was I misled.

What tended to happen in my adult life with women was that they'd find me in a broken place, and they'd try to possess me. It was as if I were an object, not a man. Of course, I'd let them, because all I knew was being broken. I didn't know what being whole felt like.

I can't say that I've had serious suicidal thoughts where I plan out how I'm going to end my life, but it was moments like that day on the 101 where I thought about just laying down and giving up. I just wanted to lay down in the middle of the street and give up. Is that the definition of suicidal? Maybe?

As Christians, we're told that suicide is like throwing away what God gave you. It's like you're buying your one-way ticket to Hell. If you feel like your life here is Hell already, then you're not going to forge your own exit to Heaven. That being said, the idea of giving up and just waiting to be swallowed by the earth is a lot easier to comprehend from the spiritual mind versus a planned death.

I'd been fighting a spiritual war with an earthly mindset, and that's why I couldn't win. I was simply ill-equipped.

It was a problem I'd had my entire life, though you don't realize the lack of ammo in your arsenal until you're actually asked to whip it out. I tried to that day, and sure enough the bullets were gone. They were never really there in the first place — I just didn't realize it until that moment.

My life has been a wild ride, littered with more ups and downs that I can even tell you...but I'll try. Some moments have been so intense that they stand as a crazy story by themselves, while other moments have played into larger ones, but the final result is always the same – I learn something. Throughout the next however many chapters, I'll walk you through this journey of mine. It's bumpy and disjointed, but it all comes together in the end. Life.

2

BECOMING HARRISON WRONG

I haven't made the best decisions in my 30+ years on this Earth, and I take responsibility for most of that. But every story starts somewhere, and maybe if I had some better footing, I could have forged a better path.

I was almost born in a Kansas City jail in 1982, but the police department had some leniency with my mother and allowed her to go to the hospital to welcome me into the world. She was awaiting a trial for shooting and killing my father, who before his death, was an officer at the Kansas City Police Department.

That might sound wild, but you'd also have to know that my father was an extremely crooked cop. He ran in the streets, he had a drug ring, a prostitution ring, and he had a whole bunch of crooked friends. My mother was the good girl dating the bad guy, and eventually it caught up to her. The funny thing is, I went 13 years of my life thinking that my father died in the line of duty in some honorable way. I'm thinking it was like a lost scene from *Braveheart* – you know, with my dad jumping in to save the day or some shit. Meanwhile, it's actually some Denzel Washington in *Training Day* type shit.

It was 1994, and we were living in a one-bedroom apartment in Inglewood, California. There was one weekend where one of my brothers had spent the weekend with his father, and when he got back, we got into one of our usual arguments. We were always fighting, yet we loved each other to death too. That's what brothers do, right?

I was holding him down and I wouldn't let him go, and he looks me in my eyes and says, "That's why Mom killed your dad!" I instantly let him go and took a step back.

"What? What did you just say?"

I didn't give him time to answer. I just walked into the living room to find my mother, where she was having an argument with my stepfather about something else.

"Mom, you killed my dad?"

It was like a vacuum came and sucked all of the air out of the room. She slowly turned away from my stepfather and looked at me with a look in her eyes that I'd never seen before.

"Keith..."

My family calls me Keith.

"...You should sit down."

My entire world stopped in that moment.

She went on to give me the most abridged version that she could, I guess taking into consideration that she was telling a 13-year-old about how she murdered his father, who was also not the man I'd thought him to be for over a decade of my life. In that moment, my whole life changed. I lost all respect for authority, for adults. The trust in everything I thought was real was not real anymore. Nothing was real.

The details don't matter now, but my mother was able to get out of jail. That's how we ended up in California; we had to be shipped out to the middle of nowhere as a part of Witness Protection. At least that's what I assume based on what I've had to piece together on my own. My family is quite the secretive type, but I guess these kinds of details aren't the type of things casually discussed at holiday dinners.

We moved around a lot in California, and after a brief time in Valencia (where I became friends with neighbors in our complex like Meagan Good and her family), we moved out to Newhall. I felt like life was pretty cool at that point. I had a clean house, a clean school, my mom was there, we stayed in church.

Church is a very important part of my story.

There was a big brother program at our church in

Inglewood, and they paired me with a man by the name of Melvin Staples. In my eyes, he couldn't have been any cooler. He had a dope car and he had his own security company that protected the big guys like James Cameron, who directed films like *Terminator* and *Titanic*. To me, Melvin was the definition of a real man, and up until that point, I hadn't really had a male figure in my life like that. My mother was married a few years prior, but that didn't work out, so it was just me, her and my little brother. It felt so healthy to have a big brother type to look up to, but that didn't last very long.

In just a short time, my mom fell in love with Melvin and ended up marrying him. It went from big bro to stepfather in a finger snap. It was a little weird at first, but ultimately, I decided that I was happy with her decision. After all, this was my guy! The feeling of having such a cool person to not only look after me but my mom as well just felt...right. But as quickly as it started, it ended, because Melvin ended up cheating on my mother with his secretary while she was pregnant with my little brother Chris. Life comes at you fast.

With the split, we ended up moving again. We hauled over to Canyon Country off my father's pension into a beautiful three-bedroom house and man, it felt like we made it. We had a treehouse in the backyard, I'm in the canyons chasing rattlesnakes, rollerblading down the sidewalks, playing street hockey and riding dirt bikes. I was on my white boy shit, and I loved every second of it. My life felt normal, even after all of the moving around we had done up until that point. For the first time in a long time, I finally felt like I was home. But just like every single pattern in my life up until that point, that feeling was fleeting and changed quickly, courtesy of an earthquake.

California gets earthquakes all the time – we know this – but this wasn't just a little tremor. The January 1994 Northridge Earthquake had a 6.7 magnitude and lasted like 10–20 seconds. That shit did some fucking damage; it was the highest ever recorded in an urban area in North America! Then the aftershocks hit. There were two, about 11 hours apart and each at 6.0 on the Richter scale. Those did even more damage.

For some real context of how extreme it was: 57 people died that day, more than 8,700 were injured, and the property damage was in the range of $13–$50 billion. Sounds like a wide margin, but so many places were affected, and repairs were costly. Parts of the I-10 and the I-5 collapsed completely, leaving them closed for a minute.

I say all of that to then say – my mom did not take to the earthquake well at all. Actually, she freaked out. I had never really seen her act like that, but the whole experience rattled her, especially because of the freeways collapsing. She was so concerned about the fact that she had three boys and could possibly be trapped up in Canyon Country and unable to move around. So, what was the remedy? Marrying the first person around who could save her from whatever situation she thought could happen.

In less than a week after the earthquake, she married a joker by the name of Richard Jones. He was the deacon at our church. I knew he wasn't good; I felt it. I want to say that I'm a spiritual empath, I can smell you out. It's been a gift since I was young, and I was quick to tell my mother that this one wasn't it. My aunts told me I was being selfish, though, so I had to take a step back and let my mom do what she was going to do.

This is the woman who was basically my first girlfriend. It was always me and her, driving in that red Toyota from Santa Clarita to Carson every day for church. On Monday we had prayer, Wednesday it was Bible study, Thursday night choir rehearsal, and Friday some type of men's meeting. Then Saturday it was always one thing or another going on there and then Sunday it was both day and night service. I stayed in church, I stayed with my mom and that's how we lived. But now that was changing.

My mother married Richard in the pastor's office, and that day, all of us moved into his one-bedroom Inglewood apartment with him. Not long after that was the aforementioned incident where I found out about what really happened to my father. The period that followed was rough, and psychologically, it took a toll on me.

Everything I'd ever known to be "true" about my life turned out to have all been built from a lie, which essentially invalidated everything I thought I knew about myself. Now I don't know who I am at all, and as my still-developing mind is attempting to process the new information about my father, I also had to process the actual fact that I was now a stranger to myself.

To grow up without a father is a disadvantaged task in and of itself. You're literally missing a piece of the puzzle that is your core foundation, so as you grow, you learn to supplement that with life experiences and information gathered from hearing stories from your family that knew him, and eventually you develop your own identity. Now after over a decade of doing so, I would have to unlearn all of that and start from the very beginning.

Try having to deal with all of that while simultaneously moving from the suburbs to the hood where now I'm the antithesis of cool. I'm well-spoken, I'm not from the streets, and I'm smarter than a lot of these guys that I'm in school with. The girls liked me because I was cute, but the guys hated me for that same reason and also because I talked like a white boy. Truth be told, it left me fighting a lot with everyone.

I had to learn to switch it up real quick, because if I didn't dumb it down and start talking like they did, I was going to keep fighting every single day. So, I did and thankfully, it started getting better.

We didn't really have money like that, but we looked like we did. My aunt Jocie had been in the military my whole life, and she would always go to the navy exchange and put together boxes of all the best jewelry, all the best shoes and all the best clothes. She kept us looking like we really had it together, and that ended up being a gift and a curse.

It was the first day back after Christmas break in 8th grade, and courtesy of Aunt Jocie, I had a brand-new pair of blue and white Deion's, a blue and white Dallas Cowboys Starter jacket with the zipper on the side and a brand-new Sony CD Walkman. You couldn't tell me that I wasn't the man that day! I felt like a million bucks as I walked out of our house! My mom told me not to take that Walkman to school that morning, but I didn't listen. I couldn't. I was so proud of what I had, and I wanted to walk home from school listening to my music.

Young Columbus

The day at school was great; everyone was jocking me! I thought I was on! Everything was cool, but then I had to walk home after school...and that included a walk through the hood.

As I walked, these two OGs I'd never seen at school before approached me.

"Aye, cuh — pull up right here! Pull up right here, cuh!" They motioned for me to stop walking and stand off to the side with them.

I had no other option but to do it. They told me that they liked what I had on, and the next thing I knew, I was on the ground with no jacket, no shoes and no Walkman.

I had to walk home barefoot with nothing but my backpack.

I walked into the house to see my stepdad looking at me with a confused look on his face. I looked butthurt and angry.

"What happened to your stuff?"

I immediately burst into tears. He could tell that I'd gotten beaten up.

"If you ever come back in this house again without your stuff, you're going to have to fight me," he said. He didn't smile, he didn't yell. He said it so calmly in a matter-of-fact tone and I knew I never wanted to fight him, so my only other option was to adhere to what he was telling me. The problem was, I had no clue how to avoid that happening again.

"But how?" I asked him through tears.

He told me that I would have to catch each one of the kids who jumped me when they were alone and give each one the work when I see them. You know, rough them up individually to return the favor and assert my stance that I was never to be fucked with again.

"They don't want you by themselves," he told me. "They can only take you in a group." So that's what I did. I cornered them alone, kicked each of their asses, and I was never stolen from again. It was the best advice he'd ever given me.

It was moments like these that gave me such complicated feelings in my heart about him. As a man, he was pretty shady, but I can't really say he didn't do his job as a father figure. This man encouraged me a lot. He was the guy at all of my football practices and all of my games, the guy playing basketball with me and training me. The emotional effects of what was going on between him and my mother were really taking a toll on me beyond any supportive act, though.

All night they would fight: doors slamming, feet stomping, lots of screaming. My two brothers would be fast asleep and I'd lay there night in and night out, listening to the two of them spiral out of control. The crazier part is, it wasn't until I was older that I really understood that he was trying to get my mom to be the woman of integrity she seemed to lack the ability to be.

But that was truly the blind leading the blind, as he would eventually prove time and time again that despite preaching God's word, he seemed to have a real loose interpretation of how to practice it.

3

YOUR PUSSY IS SHOWING

I hated my family so much, but I found family in the hood. I found solace in the hood with the gang bangers. I found support in the hood with these niggas, even though it was a bullshit lifestyle. So, what'd I do? I started thinking I was a little Crip – but an educated one!

I was legitimately hiding how much I was reading and studying and how I cared about my penmanship and my class notes. I was a phenomenal student, but I was still getting in all of this trouble in middle school because of the decisions I was making outside of the classroom. With that being said, my mom had absolutely no leniency with me when it was time to decide on a high school.

I wanted to go to Hamilton School of the Arts on the west side of L.A. It was (and still is) predominately black, and all of my friends were supposed to be going there; Meagan was supposed to be there along with the twins, Malika and Khadijah Haqq. At the time, the twins had already been working actresses like Meagan and we'd all known each other for years from growing up near each other, so it made even more sense to stick with them.

But, nah. Instead, my mother put me in El Segundo across town. It's the most racist little city in Los Angeles County. They're stuck in a time warp. It's 99.9% white.

If I thought I was a tough little Crip before, you couldn't tell me ANYTHING in El Segundo. I was walking around Cripped up from the hip up, cuh. And I was an all-around athlete on top of that? Basketball, football and track...forget it. But like I said, this is a racist ass town and so unfortunately but quite unsurprisingly, some racist ass shit went down.

Me playing football

There was this gang there called the Polar Bears, but maybe you can guess based on the name and the overall context that they were a white supremacist gang. They had members from high school kids to 20-somethings, and I ended up having to beat down one of their dumb asses in class early in the fall of my freshman year. I'm talking BEAT DOWN. We were both football players though, so the school kind of left us alone as far as suspensions and shit like that. But of course, dude wasn't going to just let it go after we fought a fair one. White boys don't honor the code.

Football practice became an issue from then on, after this kid told his little buddies on the team to stop blocking for me. I ended up having to fight everybody and cuss these little motherfuckers out all season, but that wasn't even the worst of my troubles. That was really probably the least.

By January, I'd already been suspended three times. If number four came in, I already knew that I was out of there. That was the limit. I didn't really love my school, but I wasn't trying to have that. It would come with a whole different set of problems at home and there were already more than enough there.

It's basketball season at this point and of course I'm playing on the team, so I'm at open gym one day just getting my shots up. I was there with four of our grand total of seven black kids enrolled in our school. Five of us were on the team; the other two were girls. The school had over 1,100 students.

As I was shooting around, I heard a door slam. I looked over and it was all of the Polar Bears – and I mean ALL of the Polar Bears, including alumni. I'm talking grown men that graduated years before. They all had bats and chains in-hand, and I had to really take in what I was actually witnessing. These niggas were chaining the door shut like a fucking movie. This felt like a scene out of *American History X* or something! It was really real. And they were there for ME because I fought their little dude months ago. White boys may not honor the code, but man do they have this holding a grudge shit down. Our black folks, though? We stick together, especially in the face of some racist bullshit – and that's exactly what my four boys who were shooting with me did. This may have been my battle, but they were all ready to rumble.

"You got to knock at least two of these fools out," one of the four, Jabari, said as we watched these dudes surround us. We were trying to calculate it like, "Okay yeah I could knock two of these dudes out if I move over here at this angle and then you could go here and take those two," but they had weapons and shit! I was ready to give these white boys the business, but I was also fully aware that I was ABSOLUTELY getting kicked the fuck out of school after this. Meanwhile, Jabari and a few others were standing there trying to negotiate with them. Everybody knows you can't negotiate with terrorists.

As soon as it was about to go down, the principal busted through the locker rooms or something. I couldn't exactly see where he came from, but I knew it wasn't the door that was all chained up.

"Stop! The cops are on their way, and all of you are going down!"

I legitimately have no idea how he got into the room or how he even knew it was going down, but once again, it was a scene straight out of a movie. I swear, you can't make my life up.

He handed out like seven suspensions that day, but thankfully, I wasn't one of them. And the story ends here and everything is happily ever after, right? Of course not. I'd gotten the white boys under control, but someone else was waiting in the wings to fuck up my tenure at El Segundo. (Spoiler alert: that someone was me.)

I had this English teacher by the name of Ms. Boone that year. Later on, I'll tell you about my attraction to older women, but just know that she was about 24 or 25 and fit right into that mold. And to top it off, I'd also always attracted older women since before my age was even in the double digits, so as was par for the course of my life, she was always flirting with me and Jabari.

Seriously, every day she would ask me to stay after class for something and she was just extremely touchy-feely. I'm confident if I wanted to hit it, I could have. Or at least I'd like to believe that!

I would sit in the back and talk a lot and crack jokes, so her "solution" would be to put me in the front, right in front of her. At the start of class, she'd sit on a stool with a mini-skirt with her legs open right in front of me. I'd be literally staring at her vagina every day – and sometimes it'd be sans underwear. She was really trying to put it in our faces. And by our, I mostly mean mine.

But just like kids my own age, she apparently wanted to get my attention by embarrassing me in class in front of everyone. There was one particular day that she just said something that was way more out of pocket than usual. And the way that I was built at the time, I was really the wrong one to play with.

"Ms. Boone, come on. You're tripping."

She came at me crazy again.

"Bumblebee Tuna! Your pussy is showing!"

It rolled off my tongue without even a second thought.

If you don't get the reference, you're not old enough to even be reading this book. It was a line from *Ace Ventura: When Nature Calls* where Jim Carrey's character is greeting the Wachati tribe and keeps saying "Bumblebee Tuna" thinking he's repeating their actual greeting, "Bumbawe atuna." Then he tells one of the men that his balls are showing.

The shit was hilarious in the movie, and it was even more hilarious in the classroom that day because the movie was so hot at the time. The whole class fell out as soon as I said it.

Needless to say, the same principal who had saved me from the white boys was the same person who expelled me that very same day. And the story doesn't even end there. My mother and Richard were fucking pissed to say the very least, but "lucky" for me, Richard would ultimately be the reason I'd end up in a whole different state for my sophomore year months later.

He'd promised from day one that he'd get us out of that one-bedroom apartment in the hood, and he ended up following through. We'd moved to a four-bedroom, three-story house in Harbor City during my time at El Segundo, and though our surroundings had improved, things weren't that much different behind closed doors.

I was home one day playing the drums, because the church had let me borrow their drum set. I was a drummer in the kids' choir at the time and my mom was the director, so they let me borrow the set for the week because I told them that I needed to practice. I'd learned how to play every single instrument without ever owning a single one, because I would just sit in the church and practice whenever I could. I was no longer in school at this point anyway so it's not as if I had many other things to be doing with my time.

Inglewood had taught me how to be a little more G'd up, so now I'm a lot more about it than I used to be. On this specific night, I felt like pops was wilding more than usual. I was tired of the way he spoke to my mother. I was tired of hearing the fighting. I was just tired. I stopped playing and reached down to grab one of the sharp floor tiles and went upstairs with it to the middle level of the house. I needed to handle this right here and right now.

"Come down and catch a fade with a real one!" I yelled upstairs. I was shaking like a leaf as I'd said it, but I had to be a man. I couldn't let this go down any longer. Pops comes out with a bat and ran down the stairs so fast, that all I could do was take off. I wasn't ready to hit him, and I wasn't ready to get hit either.

I ran back downstairs and finally, my brother John had woken up. This nigga was always sleeping through everything! He saw that I was getting chased by pops and he just tapped in right away. It was like I had tagged him in without saying a word, and that was just a true brotherly connection. He was two years younger than me and I literally never expected that he would just come to bat for me like that with no questions asked. John ran around the couch and was on pops' neck like a beast! He was legitimately trying to choke him and we had to tag team at that point; there was no other choice. I was so sad that it had come to that, but that's what had to be done. You better believe I ran right out of the house from there, though.

We lived around the corner from a K-Mart, so I ran to find my shoes and flew out of the house. I ran to that K-Mart as fast as I could, straight to the payphone outside. I called my grandmother collect and as soon as she picked up the phone, I spilled my heart out.

"I can't deal with this no more, Nana! I can't," I told her. "I'm either going to kill this man or he's going to kill somebody. I don't know, but something's going to happen. I have to go."

There's nothing like a grandmother's love. She told me I could go stay with her, and since I didn't even have a school I'd have to "leave," I wasn't leaving much. I was a good student, but I was acting wild in school. I didn't respect anybody, especially not authority figures, so you couldn't tell me anything.

My Nana and I

And just like that, I moved to Arizona.

4

IF YOU SEEK AMY

I lived in Arizona for a little over a year, and at 16, I came back to my live with my mom in California.

I'd done summer school the year prior in Arizona to get my academics back on point and ended up with an amazing sophomore year of high school. All it took was the right environment for me to blossom, and I was able to return to California with a renewed sense of myself and a better outlook on the world.

My mom had promised that she wasn't with my abusive stepfather anymore, so I was comfortable going back. I enrolled in the Orange County High School of the Arts, and my entire junior year was amazing. It was everything I never had before in school. Everything was finally right.

Senior year started and it was going well, and

then...there he was. I came home from school one day and my stepfather was just in the house. It could have gone a lot of ways, but I was in such a good place that I just let it ride. At that point, we'd grown so much from that infamous incident, so I figured fuck it, let's just be a family. We lived like that for about two more months before an opportunity presented itself to leave once again.

At this point, my schedule at OCHSA was academics until lunch, then my arts classes until 5 p.m. If I was doing a show, I'd be at the school until at least 10 p.m. on some nights. This was one of those nights, and when I got back to our house, it looked like the S.W.A.T. Team had taken over.

My brother happened to page me at that same exact moment, and I knew something was really wrong. He used the code that we had come up with to let each other know when there was an emergency, so I rushed to call him and it turned out that our mother was in the hospital because she'd gotten into a fight with my joker of a step-father. To add insult to injury, he stole her car that night as well.

Dealing with my anger was always an issue for me, but for some time I'd managed to keep it at bay. In that moment, all of those feelings came back in full force and I really wanted to kill him for real. Somehow I managed to keep my composure and instead, I turned right around and booked it to my then-girlfriend's house.

When I walked in with tears in my eyes, she handed me a copy of the *Backstage West* magazine that was sitting on her coffee table and told me to go through it. The first thing I saw when I opened it was that *STOMP*, the touring off-Broadway "physical theatre" show, was holding open auditions in San Francisco the following week. That was all I needed to see. By this point I had my own car, my own money; I was like the black Zack Morris at OCHSA. So if I wanted to go, I could go — and I wanted to go.

I drove myself to San Fran with my uncle Robert without even telling my mom what we were doing or where we were going. We both auditioned and took the drive back, and we both made it into the finals. The call came when we were already back in L.A., so once again we hit the 5 and made that drive to the Bay. On this round, they narrowed it down to 30 people, but they only needed six for the show. The other 24 would be put on a waiting list and that's where I landed.

This was before the days it was normal for someone my age to have a cell phone, and I couldn't give them my home number to contact me because if they spoke to my mom, they'd find out I wasn't actually 18 yet. Instead, I gave them an admin number at OCHSA and made the drive back down to L.A. once again.

Two weeks later I got called into the office at school, and I was thinking that I was in trouble. Instead, they tell me that I have a call and now I'm thinking that something bad happened. It wasn't anything bad at all. I got into *STOMP!*

I had been trying to find a way out, and here was my ticket. Never mind the fact that I had a 3.8 GPA and was planning to attend either Julliard, New York University, Boston Conservatory or Berkeley School of Music – damn near every school a creative could ever dream of attending. I was the equivalent of what a number one NFL high school prospect would be in the arts world. So while yes, I was ready to go to college, I wanted to get the hell out of my house right then and there.

With that said, it was on. I am forever grateful that I had the support that I did at OCHSA, because they created these packets that allowed me to finish school in six weeks from the road. (I didn't care about walking, so later I got my diploma and that was it. I came back for prom, though.)

The process happened so fast and it was such a whirlwind. I was supposed to rehearse for six weeks, but after just two, they threw me into the show. At the age of 17, I was now touring the world. Three years prior, I was playing drums in my basement and coming to blows with my stepfather, and now I'm being paid to do what I love and meet people around the globe. I didn't think life could be greater, and then God stepped in like, "I got you, little homie. Watch this."

Fast forward to July 31, 2001, where we were doing our final show of that leg of the tour in Tampa, Florida. I was high as a giraffe's tail, rolling on ecstasy with the rest of the cast, and we walked into a 7-Eleven at like 2:30 in the morning. I saw a cardboard cutout of Britney Spears outside to advertise her upcoming world tour and right there, I said it.

"I'm going to choreograph for her one day," I confidently told the crew. They laughed, but I was dead serious. "I promise y'all, I'm going to be her choreographer."

We went our separate ways after that, because for the first time in a year and a half, we finally had our first break. They pay you for seven weeks, but you go home and regroup during that time, so I came home and immediately used my money to rent a house. I moved a few other dancers in to help me with the rent, and I would watch them every day. I wasn't as good as them, and I needed to be better.

I'd started taking classes every day—four or five a day for at least two weeks—when the Britney audition came. Wade Robson was the choreographer, and I was confident I was already in there because my friend and future business partner, Kevin Tancharoen, was his assistant. I just knew I had it in the bag with ease. God set me up for this moment, and I'd spoken it into existence!

Nope. Got cut on the first round.

Surprisingly enough, this didn't discourage me. In fact, it only fired me up. I wanted to get back into my classes with a vengeance, come back and stunt on everyone. I was still going to work with Britney in the future. There was no doubt in my mind.

I was in classes every day still, and a few weeks later, one of my buddies whose class I was taking had to go to the Philippines. For whatever reason, he asks me to be the sub for his class at Millennium, and I couldn't even understand why.

"Me?" I asked him. "I'm still learning, bro. Are you serious?"

He was serious. He just handed me his class, and just like that, I was a teacher. At the same time, Kevin and I had started working together on music production, and things were really starting to take off. I'm in classes all day now and in the studio at night, producing and writing music for whoever wants it. We worked closely with a teenager named Jhené Aiko around that time, and we helped Diddy with his new girl group project, a group named Dream. Kevin was dating Dream's lead singer back then, so we actually worked on their entire album.

Diddy, Mos Def, Q-Tip and Myself

Fun fact to randomly throw in: I was actually married through all of this time. It was a quick marriage at 19, right when I came back from *STOMP*. I was still very much involved in our church, and they made me feel like marriage was a must to truly live the life of a saved man. Oh, and apparently I wasn't a man of God because I had locks in my hair.

A logical person could have easily brushed off what the church was saying, especially because I really didn't want a wife. I'm 19, I have a life to live. But God was the only man who had ever really been there for me, and I felt like I had to not only please Him, but the people at my church as well. So what do I do? I cut off my hair and I married the girl.

So here I am, dread-less and married and putting in more work than I'd ever had. In between classes and the studio at night with Kevin, I'm also working at Bally's Total Fitness to help with the bills and there literally weren't enough hours in the day. I wasn't sleeping; I was grinding.

Kevin and I

It was soon after that I met Jamie King at Millennium, and he really took to me. This man has worked with Michael Jackson, Madonna, basically any and all of the biggest names out, and he liked *my* work. I could feel that he was going to help me in one way or another, but I didn't even realize how fast it was going to happen.

He puts me on a Nike gig that he was the Creative Director for, and Lisette Bustamante and Chonique Sneed were the choreographers. We toured a few cities, and as we were on the way back to Los Angeles, Jamie told me that I have the night to re-pack and get back on a plane the following day.

"I need you in Chicago tomorrow," he told me. "We're doing Oprah."

"We? We *who*?" I questioned. I wasn't even trying to be funny; I was legitimately confused. "Who is *we*?"

"Madonna has her *Fall into the Gap* campaign, and Punch is on another gig. I need you to take his spot."

Punch was one of my best brothers from Kansas City, and he had gotten another gig with either Brandy or Mariah Carey at the time, so I was more than happy to fill his shoes. I didn't even hesitate before telling him I'd do it, and little did I know that he was actually testing me.

We get to the Chi the following day, and he took me right to Harpo and put me in the back of the room. All of the veteran choreographers in the game were in that room: I'm talking Leo Moctezuma, Gil Duldulao, like eight of these heavy-hitters. Huge names in the dance industry. And me.

Jamie looked me dead in my eyes and said, "Columbus, you got 15 minutes. I need eight eight-counts right now. Teach them."

If you were only given one word to describe the personalities of choreographers, catty would be the one. If you were to look up the definition of catty in the dictionary, a photo of choreographers would accompany it. So here is a rookie of all rookies, coming in and being given the reigns to teach a handful of the best in the business. You can imagine the tone in the room. But as I always have done, I rose to the occasion and we had an amazing show.

The very next day, Jamie told me that he'd gotten hired to direct for Britney Spears' new tour, and that he wanted four numbers from me for it. Lisette and Chonique had been tapped as the lead choreographers, but he knew what I could bring to the table and I knew I would kill it. I told y'all I was going to land Britney. Manifestation is fucking real.

And man, did I land Britney...

5

"WHY ARE YOU FUCKING THAT
NIGGER?!"

I'd signed on to be a background dancer for Britney, but Jamie gave me four numbers that I was going to be able to choregraph myself. As soon as I was back in L.A., rehearsals started, and I didn't even get time to tell Kevin that I'd landed the gig. I was straight into work mode and though we were in touch here and there to discuss the work we were doing together, the topic of me working with Britney had still yet to come up.

While I was in the middle of rehearsal one day, he called me and told me that our production company, The Tekniks, had a "big" session that I needed to come in for immediately. He refused to tell me who it was for, though.

I made it down to the studio pretty quickly, but I took a break outside first to smoke a cigarette when I heard a woman's voice on the other side of the gate.

"I'm at the gate!"

I knew that voice. I was almost positive that it was Felicia, Britney's assistant. Kevin had produced for that last Britney tour I didn't make the cut for, and I'd gone and visited him a few times on the road so I'd built a rapport with a lot of her team. Since then, Wade Robson had fucked Britney and told Justin Timberlake about it, so all of that shit was going down.

Britney Spears and I performing

Keep that in mind as you hear the rest of this story.

The gate opened and there was Felicia, Britney's security team, and of course, Britney. Through his previous work with Britney when he was Wade's assistant, Kevin had been hired to do all the remixes for a show that she had coming up – and her team had no idea that he and I were production partners. As we all stood there looking at each other, everyone was equally as confused at the small world connection and excited as we all realized we were about to work together.

"Wait, you're a producer too?" Britney asked me.

"Yep."

"AND a choreographer?"

"Yep!"

She didn't believe me at first, so Kevin was quick to pull up a few videos of some of the choreography we'd done as a team. Let me tell y'all, your girl was impressed. But, that's not what we were there for that night.

We put her in the studio and we remixed everything. Her manager at the time, Larry Rudolph, ended up popping up later that night with Britney's brother, and at one point, the topic turned to her next single. Larry was pushing this R. Kelly collaboration called "Outrageous," and Britney was NOT fucking with it. They were both on Jive at the time, and apparently the label had made a deal with Kells that he'd have Britney's next single. But the go-to "it" production duo Red Zone had produced "Me Against the Music" for her, and that's what she really wanted to go with.

"They're not listening to me, Columbus!" Britney said to me. Her voice was cracking and she was either about to start crying or her twang was just making the whole thing sound more dramatic.

Whatever it was, I already knew what she could do.

"Larry, hear me out," I told him. "Didn't Britney just kiss Madonna at the MTV Awards?"

Obviously, the answer was yes.

"Put Madonna on the record, and it's gone. It's out of here!"

That was all I had to say. Britney loved the idea immediately, and even Larry was on board. Brit pushed for someone to call Madonna right then and there, so Larry did. And just like that, Madonna was coming to rehearsal the next day to see what we were doing.

It's really crazy how you can go days, weeks, months, even years with nothing. No hope, no signs of something better to come, and yet in the blink of an eye, every single thing can change and just keep changing and keep growing. Less than 24 hours later, Madonna was recording her part, and we were already discussing video treatments. The label was excited, but now they were looking at the grand scheme of things. In their minds, it made no sense to be outsourcing Lisette, Chonique and Jamie when they already had me and Kevin in-house to do the music and the choreography.

So, what did they do? They fired all three of them.

It was honestly a logical move, but from the outside looking in, it looked crazy. I didn't sleep with Britney, I didn't get in anyone's ear; it was merely logistics, but Lisette and Chonique weren't trying to hear that. They were HURT and I get it, but they really went out for blood. They started telling the entire dance industry that I was sleeping with Britney and all kinds of things, and literally started to get me blackballed from the whole industry. It was that serious.

To be stopped from doing what you love and making money is hard enough in itself, but maybe it would have been a slightly easier pill to swallow if it was something that was actually my fault. I was being blackballed over something that wasn't even true! Mentally this was beyond draining, but at the same time, I still had this gig with Britney. No matter what people were saying, God still reserved my blessings for me. It takes a lot of self-discipline to ignore the outside chatter and just focus on the goal, but I had to lock in. What was for me wasn't about to pass me.

Once the smoke cleared out, Jamie called me up and we had a real conversation. I explained everything, and he was really cool about it. He understood that I really didn't have anything to do with what had happened and how it all went down, and he gave me his blessings. I really appreciated that. When all was said and done, he realized that I was just a young kid chasing a dream and taking opportunities when they present themselves. I wasn't trying to shit on anyone to get ahead, and the game just plays out like it plays out sometimes. To this day, I appreciate that he put his ego to the side and chose to meet the moment with positivity. If only Chonique had kept that same energy.

Chonique was really upset, and ultimately it came down to the fact that she was embarrassed to come back to Los Angeles empty-handed after the biggest gig of her career. How do you explain to people that the rookie Columbus got your gig? You tell everyone that he was fucking Britney, because a lie is more convenient on the ego than what the truth was.

She was planting the seeds into the ears of whoever would listen, and with a rumor as juicy as a backup dancer fucking one of the biggest superstars at the time, people ate it up. It wasn't affecting my business with Britney, however, so it was manageable at the time. But months later, I believe these early seeds gave "credibility" to similar, stronger rumors that would go on to REALLY keep me from eating. More on that later, though.

I turned 21 on September 19; a few weeks after being officially added to Britney's team. Kevin and I had been working all night in the studio on this particular day, when Britney called us to tell us she needed us and our dancers in New York right away. She was about two months out from dropping her *In The Zone* album and had started full-steam ahead on the promotional portion of it.

She sent us a jet, and just like that, we were in New York having a wild party for my 21st birthday. Britney was staying in Keith Richards' apartment uptown at the time, and we were all in there going crazy. But she was going even more crazy. She was on me like white on rice, and would not leave me alone the entire night. Britney had her eyes on the prize and wasn't about to stop until she got what she wanted.

Luckily, I'm a pro. I was young but I knew what I was doing, and to keep it all the way real, I wasn't really attracted to her like that. I knew the real her, and that was enough for me to know that we should keep it professional. On top of that, I was separated from my first wife and dating another one of Brit's backup dancers at the time, Stephanie Moseley — may she rest in peace.

At one point in the night, Britney pulled me aside and told me that she needed me to come to Rome with her so she could prepare for the "Me Against the Music" video, but I thought it'd be a better idea to send Kevin. I could work with the dancers on this side, and Kevin could follow up overseas. But she wasn't having it.

"No, I want you," she told me. But I knew better. Kevin

had already told me that Britney liked me, and he very clearly cautioned me not to take the bait.

"Whatever you do, Short, don't fuck her! That's the shit that fucked the last tour," he'd warned. "Whatever you do, do not fuck that girl." His words kept replaying in my head.

I promised I wouldn't, and I had every plan to stick to that promise, despite being worn down and agreeing to go with her to Rome. It was just Britney, her security team and me, because she was doing the Pepsi commercial with Beyoncé and Pink. She wanted to be caught up to date with the choreography because she knew she was going to be doing the video when she got back to L.A. and she didn't want to come back trying to play catch-up.

In my mind, the plan was that we were going to get this work done and keep it at that. That really, truly was the plan. At least it was for me.

Funny thing about plans, though...

I really tried my best, but this girl put on the full-court press. Britney knew what she was doing! I was there like a scared kid, knowing that I shouldn't do it – not only because Kevin specifically told me not to, but more importantly because my fucking girlfriend was on the tour! The thing was, I really wanted to keep my job and I felt like if I didn't do what she wanted, I wasn't going to have a job when we got back home.

We ended up being intimate that one time. I never

slept with her again after that, though. I knew I couldn't keep something like that going; it was in literally no one's best interest. This was a dangerous sexual alliance for every reason under the sun, and I think the worst part of it was that I was making the rumors an actual reality.

When we got back to the U.S., Britney ended up moving both me and Kevin into the Trump Towers. The dancers were staying at the Mayflower around the corner, so my girlfriend would sneak over to spend the night — but Britney didn't know. The whole time, Brit was still trying to get a repeat of what happened in Rome, and she started to get suspicious because I continued to curve her. I was trying everything in the book, but really leaning on the "not wanting to convolute our creative relationship" vibe. And more than anything, I didn't want Kevin to find out what had happened. Or Stephanie.

About a week of this back-and-forth goes on and now we're on the plane coming back from the "Me Against the Music" video. Timing may seem unreal but trust me in this world, things moved very fast. Anyway, the dancers were flying commercial, but me, Britney and Kevin were on Britney's jet. And we both had our girlfriends on there too. At this time, Kevin was dating another one of Brit's dancers named Penny, and Penny was best friends with Steph, so we were able to get them both on without Britney thinking that it was because she was my girlfriend.

Britney wanted to play "Truth or Dare," because it was her new obsession, courtesy of Madonna. I felt like it wasn't going to end well but at that point, I had no other choice but to play. It stayed light and cute at first, so I figured we were in the clear. By we, I meant me.

We land, and Britney had another idea.

"You know what I want to do tomorrow after rehearsal?" she asked with almost a mischievous tone. "Let's go do hookah!" I loved the idea, thinking it was going to be the whole crew. She tells me that she just wants it to be me, her, Kevin, Penny and Steph. I knew something was up.

Falling into place

At this point, shit was already super-hot in the press. Publicity was getting crazy because I kept being pictured next to Britney, and somehow, they kept catching us in the worst moments. A simple hug would look like a kiss, a quick store run would look like a date. And though the press didn't have any intel on the rumors that Chonique had spread, I believe that the hearsay she created built a solid enough foundation among our peers that these tabloid stories completely "validated" her claims.

Britney's manager Larry was growing more upset with the continued press, and on top of that, her parents were NOT happy. The night before we went for hookah, I was next to her while she was on the phone with them crying while she had it on speaker.

"Why are you fucking that nigger?"

Britney looked at me so apologetically, knowing I'd heard it. I shook my head and didn't say anything, because what was there to say? She's a little white girl from Louisiana who was her family's golden ticket; I honestly wouldn't expect anything different.

"Mama, he's just my choreographer," she told them. "He's just my creative director!"

They weren't having that. So, this is the climate when we go to hookah the following night. Once again, Britney wanted to play Truth or Dare. And I can smell it — something was about to go all the way left. It was Penny's turn, and she asked Britney to pick a truth or a dare. Britney picked truth, and Penny asked, "When was the last time you had sex?"

Now remember, we've been together every single day for the last seven days working.

"I think seven days ago," Britney replied after thinking about it for a second.

I can see the numbers starting to crunch in everyone's head. One week ago would put us in Rome and there weren't many men that she would have had access to. I'm starting to sweat, but I figured there was a way out. Britney used to fuck Maxwell all the time, so I quickly jumped in to divert the attention.

"Man, come on. Y'all know that was Maxwell!" I told them. Britney didn't say anything. "Don't ask her no more questions because y'all already know."

That actually worked, and I was in the clear. Now it was Kevin's turn, and again, the question went to Britney.

"Britney, if you could marry one man in this world right now, who would it be?"

This is an easy one. I shouldn't have a problem here. She wouldn't dare say me, right?

"Columbus."

My jaw fell off of my face. I was trying to read the room and I wasn't getting too much, when the same question gets floated to Stephanie. What do you think her answer was? You guessed it. Me.

Now it was my turn to answer, and Kevin was doing his own internal investigation, so he asked me the very same question. This was the era of T-Mobile Sidekicks, so

I was texting him under the table asking him to stop. Yet clearly he wouldn't, so I had to play ball.

I have a really hard time just bold face lying, so I had to say who I really would — and that was Stephanie.

Bad. Move.

The second the words left my lips, I knew I'd made a mistake. Britney picked up her champagne flute and chugged the rest. As she was starting to stand up and gather herself, she put the flute down and looked up at me, demanding that I take her home immediately. But Larry had just finished telling me that I had to cool it being around Brit publicly, so I had a reason to say no. Unfortunately, that reason wasn't good enough for her.

"Columbus, drive me home NOW."

What was I going to do? I had no choice. I got the keys to her brand-new, all white SL Mercedes drop-top and told her I would bring her home. I told Kevin to follow me so that I could just drop her off and hop into his car, so he followed behind with Penny and Steph in the car. I really wanted to avoid being seen by paparazzi because we really were a team with Larry and I cared about what he said. More importantly, I cared about Britney. We were trying to wrangle that girl! She kept getting her hands on drugs at the time and we were all trying to figure out where it was coming from because she was a mess.

I was so conflicted as I drove her down Ocean Boulevard, knowing the potential disaster I had on my hands. It was ultimately a lose-lose and unless a miracle was about to shine down on me, I was going to be cooked. If I played nice and kept Britney at bay, the paparazzi would continue to capture this façade of us being a thing – thus continuing the hit to my career. If I stood my ground and created the boundaries with her that I needed to, she was liable to do or say anything...which could also be a hit to my career. And my relationship.

Naturally, the paparazzi were out there and captured us in the car. Just my luck. We pulled up to the front of her place and I turned to her.

"I'ma have to say bye here, Brit. I'll see you at rehearsal tomorrow." I reached for a hug, but she was still trying.

"Columbus," she said, grabbing me, "Come upstairs!"

I think in another circumstance I would have just obliged, but we were too far gone now. Management was on us, paparazzi was ready, Steph was in the car behind us. I just couldn't.

I got out and got into Kevin's car and we sped off. I was fired not too long after that, and Britney changed her number so I couldn't contact her. From the outside, it looked like I really did something to Brit. If I thought I was blackballed when I first got the gig with her, it was nothing compared to what I was about to face.

I like to take a lesson from everything that I do, especially when things go wrong. There's always a blessing that comes from a lesson derived from a bad circumstance. Sometimes the lesson is really hard to figure out and maybe it won't present itself for years to come. In this particular situation, the answer was really quite clear: don't shit where you eat, even if you really have to go.

6

WHAT A DICK

L et me take you back a bit to give you some further insight into my mindset. Even in my teens, I was always so goal-oriented and about work. While everyone else was out there chasing women—more specifically, *pussy*—I was focused on getting to auditions and getting to class on time. I really, really wanted to work.

I knew what I wanted and I knew what I could be, so what was the point of wasting time? My goals were different, my dreams were different, my vision was different, my passion and focus and discipline were very much different from my contemporaries growing up.

The craziest part is, I was built like this with no actual encouragement from home. Most kids who hit the stage at a young age have one parent or both parents pushing them to work or at the very least, praising them for their talents. I didn't grow up in a family where your mom is always telling you how great, talented and amazing you are. It was always more like, "Why are you doing that?"

With legends

Funny enough, the moment my mother realized that her kid was booking everything he went out on, suddenly she wanted to be my manager. It was around my junior year of high school that I really started going up, fresh back from Arizona and honing my craft at OCHSA. I had like four national commercials that year — a Busta Rhymes Mountain Dew commercial, a Denny's commercial, some bank and a Toyota commercial. As a self-made young actor, I naturally knew nothing about the business or residuals, but I did know that the $2700 I got from Mountain Dew was enough to be used as the down payment to my first car. I felt like I was really doing something, but my bubble would burst soon thereafter.

According to my "momager," I didn't really have any money. She was, of course, in control of my finances and was sure to remind me that I have nothing to tap into every time I was stressed that my pockets were tapped out. But shit wasn't adding up to me. How am I on all of these commercials and I'm this broke? Maybe this business really isn't all that it's cracked up to be, and if that's the case, I might need to figure out a new lane.

That changed quickly one day, though. I was in my mother's room looking for something, when I came across this big ol' ledger book with all of these copies of checks from like the whole year. The amount I was seeing started to make me dizzy. First check I find, it says $5,000. Okay, maybe something happened and it didn't go through? I don't know. I turn the page and I see another check for $4,000. Nah, this is getting weird. I keep turning — $2,000 here, $5,000 there, $3,000 there. I started doing the math for the entire year, and I ended up at a cool five figure number. MY money for ME, nowhere to be found or accounted for. I couldn't wait for her to get home, and when she did, I didn't waste a second.

"Hey ma, let me ask you something," I started. "Where are all these checks?"

"You know I put all that money away for you!" she tells me without skipping a beat, but she's visibly shaken. "You can't have all that money right now! I can't even touch that money!"

She knew that she was lying, I knew that she was lying, and she knew that I knew that she was lying. My mom had spent all of that money. There were so many things I'd needed at the time that I was struggling with – my car note, my cell phone bill. And there would be my mom telling me that I didn't have the money, when all along it was because she was spending it! Don't even get me started on the fact that from childhood, I was basically working for everybody else. I was the breadwinner for everyone. Little Keith always took care of things that no one else could, and it turns out that I was helping even more than I already knew.

From that moment on, I took control of my finances. And yet, my stepfather found a way to piss in my Cheerios yet again. Still.

It was the day before I was leaving for *STOMP* (obviously against my mother's wishes), and I really couldn't wait to go and make money that she wouldn't be able to touch. However, she kept pushing me and pushing me to open a bank account. This woman really always wanted something to do with my money! I knew I needed one, though, so I let her have my stepfather open one "for me" with $1,200 I had to deposit. The next day, I was off to San Francisco to work.

This is what I do

I was so happy to be in another city so far away from everyone. I felt like the world was mine! It was just like wow, I have a dream job, there is no one around to police me anymore and I can just live the life I've always wanted. The feeling was damn near intoxicating. I truly was so empowered. But of course, that didn't last long because when did anything great in my life last for very long?

I'd been in San Fran for a couple of days at this point. I'd started rehearsals that Monday, and then that Thursday, I went to the bank to tap into my cool little $1,200 because my castmates and I were off from rehearsals on

Friday and we wanted to enjoy our night. So, here I go strolling into the bank all jolly and ready for my night, only to find out that there was a lien on my account and it was fucking closed. My $1,200 was nowhere to be found.

How the fuck is there a lien? What even is a lien? Where did this lien come from?

I didn't know anything at this point, so I started questioning the tellers for more information. Turns out, my stepfather had a lien for failure to pay child support. Apparently, Richard had years of back child support for the kids he'd fathered prior to getting with my mom, and because his name was on my account since I was under 18 and he opened it for me, they came for my account.

The more fucked up part is that we wouldn't be paid for the first two weeks of rehearsals, so I was really shit out of luck. My $1,200 would never see the light of day again – and Richard knew that from the moment he took it out of my hands. He sent me a little $300 via Western Union to hold me over in the meantime, but fuck that $300. It was one quarter of MY hard-earned money that I had plans for, and he just used me for all of it. It was just another demerit on the chapter of him being in my life. These folks really couldn't get it right – him or my mother.

I wish I could say that was the last time he fucked up my situation. I know I've had my share of issues, but I can also say that I have way too big of a heart and forgive people too easily. I have a bad habit of giving folks way too many chances to keep fucking me over.

Throughout the years that followed, Richard would come in and out of my mom's life, and each time, he'd really appear to have changed. Many, many moons later during another one of his reappearances, he proved once again that he was still the same person when I gave him yet another shot to prove me wrong. By this point I was already married with kids, and I'd written a short film that the amazing Will Packer was actually financing. Will had $50,000 toward the project, and I was so ready for it to come together!

Part of the script called for a location that I thought my mother's house would be perfect for, so I called her and got the okay – although Richard was actually charging me to use the crib. I thought that was super weak, but cool. We have the money, I want this location – I made it happen. Whatever.

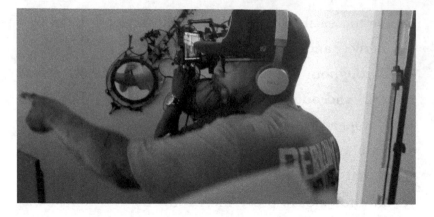

Me Directing

Everything was in full swing, and I showed up to shoot at my mom's house on this particular day with my whole 50-person crew. What do I find upon our arrival? A sheriff and my mother outside of the door. It turned out that my stepfather hadn't paid the rent in a solid five months and the landlord—who, by the way, was an old family friend—had locked them out.

Welcome to the life and times of Columbus gat damn Short.

I started panicking and scrambling to figure something out because I have my ENTIRE crew there. We were losing money by the minute and at the end of the day, despite the fact that I didn't physically cause the issue, the problem fell on my shoulders. Thank God the landlord was really cool with us. I ended up being able to call him and give him the $1,000 that I was planning to give to my stepfather to use the house, and we were able to shoot.

That was officially the last time my mom saw my stepdad. He got in his car that night, drove away and disappeared, never to return again. That was a really tough night for me after we wrapped. But yet the saying in the business is really true: the show must go on. I had another day of filming the next day and I had to get back home and prep for it, so I really didn't have time to sit there and actually take in the events of that day.

I'll never forget that feeling in my stomach when my crew finished loading out and all I saw was my mother in the garage packing boxes all by herself. It was heartbreaking. She kept insisting that she was fine, even though I knew that she wasn't. I wish I had more in me to really talk her through that night or help in some way, but I just couldn't carry something that heavy that night. My punk ass stepfather wasn't seen or heard from again for another ten years.

I know this woman had caused me pain and suffering over the years with her poor choices, but she was still my mother at the end of the day. She was a human being and regardless of what we went through, I loved her. It truly boiled my blood seeing Richard take her power from her time and time again.

The next and last time I saw Richard, it was because my stepsister had died. He had two kids from a prior relationship, my stepsister Carrie and my stepbrother Tyree, who was the same age as my little brother Chris. About three years ago, Carrie passed away at a really young age and needless to say, it was not an easy time at all.

The crazy part about running into Richard was that despite everything that had transpired over the years, it was actually really cool to be able to catch up with him. We were reminiscing on a lot of the good old times and we had some great laughs. At the same time, I was just sad, thinking, "Damn, this is a grown ass man who really just can't get right." And I feel like my mother was (and still is) exactly the same in that sense, and that's why they really couldn't instill too much in us. How are you going to teach your kids to be better when you can't even do better for yourselves? Leading by example is a real thing, and there certainly wasn't any example for myself or my siblings.

The Bible says to judge someone by their fruit. A good tree can't produce bad fruit, and a bad tree can't produce good fruit. My fruits are solid! Denzel, Ayala and Jalen – I lead by example. And with Jalen, my first born, I had a nice ten solid years coaching him on the football field and in real life. I've always been in his head, telling him to be great! And that's why he knows how to be great! Ayala, she's going to be a force to be reckoned with in this world. Denzel right now is the sharpest thing I have ever seen anywhere. You can't compare your kids, but I named him Denzel for a reason (which I will delve into later!)

Richard definitely was a character in my life, and I will give him credit and say that he changed some things for the positive. But more often than not, his toxic traits and behaviors overpowered any of those things, and I can confidently say that I picked up on some of that. I know I can't blame one person for all of my issues and I don't; it was definitely bigger than Richard. But when I reflect on moments like these, it gives me even more fuel to want to be a better father to my kids.

I will continue to break that cycle of toxicity for mine.

7

BLAARON SORKIN

There was this really interesting limbo in my career around early to middle 2006 where it was like, everything was in the can but nothing was in the theaters yet. My career was on fire and I was booking back to back projects, and at this particular point, it was the calm before the storm. I was so ready for it to rain. This is what I'd been working toward my entire life, and my season was finally here! I felt like God had given me a second chance to get it right, and I wasn't going to drop the ball again. In an expression of gratitude, I stopped smoking and drinking and focused my energy on being a "good Christian;" whatever that meant.

Accepted, Save the Last Dance 2, and *Stomp the Yard* were filmed and ready to go. I was really excited, but at the same time, none of those films looked like they were really going to move the needle like I wanted. None of those were putting my name in a Denzel Washington conversation, but when I got back from filming *Stomp the Yard*, an opportunity presented itself that looked like it would move that damn needle all the way. I got the job as a recurring cast member on a new NBC show called *Studio 60 on the Sunset Strip* with motherfucking Tommy Schlamme and Aaron Sorkin. And the cast? Matthew Perry, D.L. Hughley, Sarah Paulson, Bradley Whitford. This was the big leagues.

My favorite place

The show was a spin-off of *Saturday Night Live* with Aaron as the head writer, with the premise that we're behind-the-scenes of a live sketch comedy show called *Studio 60* (a la, *SNL*). Basically, it was a show within a show. My character, Darius Hawthorne, was a stand-up comedian who got hired as the assistant writer to Matthew Perry's character Matt. Out of the gate, there was a bidding war between CBS and NBC before we even started filming that ended in NBC agreeing to a "near-record license fee," so I truly felt confident that this show was going to be the one for me.

I mean, look at the cast alone! Then throw in the fact that I'd be adding in more reinforcement as my films start dropping back to back to back? I'm out of here! *Studio 60* premiered in September of 2006, about a month after *Accepted* dropped, a month before *SLD2* was dropping and four months before *Stomp the Yard*. This was my time.

With such a heavyweight cast like that and myself still being somewhat of a rookie, you'd think maybe a fellow black castmate would be the one to take me under his wing. It actually turned out to be Matthew Perry. It wasn't D.L. Hughley who told me to come cool out in his big King Kong trailer instead of my little one; it was Matthew. "My trailer is your trailer," he told me. Matthew Perry! (But for the record, D.L. has been more of an advocate and supportive brother to me than most in this crazy game!)

No one on set knew that I had done *Stomp the Yard*. It wasn't a secret, but I just kept it quiet because I figured none of these heavy-hitters would care about some black dance movie that I did. The topic was about to come up, though, because 14 episodes in, I had to leave to do the press junket for *Stomp the Yard* in New York City.

By now, *Studio 60* was not picking up the steam that everyone thought it would, but I honestly had faith that it was going to win. Maybe I was being ignorant, but I believed in it.

I got the approval to leave for the junket, on the condition that I made it back in time for episode 115. Easy call. I hit New York and did all the young, cool shit — *106 & Park*, radio, all of it. I wrapped that and got right back on the plane to L.A., and what happened there is exactly why I decided to add "writer" to my resume.

As I walked to my first-class seat in 1A, I put my things down and who did I see getting comfortable in 1B? Aaron fucking Sorkin with his laptop open! He asked me what the fuck I was doing there, but I had to ask the same thing. I don't know if he was actually asking a rhetorical question or if he'd planned that chance meeting, but it ended up being an important moment for my life.

Before I went to sleep for the entire cross-country flight, I noticed that the Final Draft document Aaron was working on said "Episode 115" at the top, but had nothing else on it. This is the episode that I was flying home to do the table read for and it wasn't even written yet! But hey, that wasn't really my problem.

I closed my eyes, and the next time I opened them, they were asking the passengers to set their seats upright for landing. I happened to glance over at Aaron's screen — 62 pages done. In five hours, Aaron had written a full, 62-page script for episode 115. And we read it at the table read the very next morning. Right there I decided I have to be the black Aaron Sorkin moving forward. This man exemplifies greatness!

NAACP Image Awards

I mean, this man has so many classic credits to his name — *A Few Good Men, The West Wing*, multiple hits on Broadway! If you can't write like Aaron, do not speak to me! His dialogue, his pace. It was actually through Aaron and Tommy that I learned the speed that I'm supposed to speak at, and I went on to bring that to *Scandal* later. I set the tone on *Scandal* with that, and Shonda made it a mandate after that for everyone to talk at my pace. I did that and you can fact-check that. And that all came from Aaron!

As I mentioned, the show wasn't doing well and the next morning at the table read, everyone looked completely broken. I swear, I thought somebody had died the way that it looked in that room. And in all honesty, there was a death, but it wasn't a person; it was the show. The show was dying and none of us could save it.

We really did start off okay in September – decent enough viewers that by October, NBC ordered three more scripts on top of the 13 they'd ordered. By November, we got picked up for a full 22-episode season – but the ratings just kept dipping lower and lower. Despite all types of cool little accolades that they were throwing at us like landing at No. 6 on *New York Daily News'* "Series of the Year" list, being named "Best Overall New Program" from a poll by *Broadcasting and Cable,* all that kind of shit, we were a sinking ship. The silver-lining is that the death gave me my second great Spielberg moment.

While we were in the table read for episode 115, everyone was looking sad except Sarah. She actually had a look in her eyes like, "Fuck this I'm ready to go anyway." I could read everybody, and it was Matthew who was really taking it tough. This was supposed to be his hit.

Aaron somberly walked to the head of the table,

looked around, and like the consummate leader he is, he says, "Listen guys. I know you're all a bit upset, but people love the show. Trust me when I say that."

The thing was, I wasn't upset. I was not Matthew, D.L., Bradley or Sarah. I didn't have that much equity in this show; little emotional equity, a few weeks of artistic equity and damn sure no financial equity other than the $15,000 I was getting paid every week that I was working as a recurring.

The table's silent as Aaron goes on to say, "I'm just going to say this, and then we get to work.

"Everybody you want to be watching the show is watching the show. Who cares if it gets cancelled? They are watching."

I knew who he was talking about because he told me on the plane that Spielberg was a big fan and watched every episode. And who cares about the world when Dad is watching? (One of my first movies was *War of The Worlds,* and I remember the back of his director's chair was simply labeled, "Dad." I've referred to him as that ever since.)

Dad is the perfect name for Spielberg for me, because he is a big reason why I wanted to make movies. I studied every film he wrote, produced or directed. And then to work with him and get the opportunity to sit and spend time with him one on one, was life changing. I mean he's Steven freaking Spielberg!

I can't speak for everyone in the room, but for me, hearing those words from Aaron resonated very powerfully. He meant what he said — the right people were watching the right talent at the right time — but it also meant that we were definitely getting cancelled. So, I got ahead of it, and quit before that could happen. They didn't want me to go, but I knew I had to move on and hit the dusty trail.

I had a movie coming out and my career was starting to head in a different direction. That show was really where I got my accents and dialects together, though, so every second of it was worth it for me; even if it didn't move the needle like I thought it would. The show ended up being cancelled soon after. It's still Aaron's only show that didn't get renewed. Arguably one of his best!

Lucky for me, *Stomp the Yard* ended up blowing up upon its release. It was the week of January 17, 2007, and we were up against *Alpha Dog*'s premiere, and Ben Stiller's *Night at the Museum*, which had been killing the box office for three weeks before that. We knocked everyone out of the park and not just on opening weekend, but the following week as well! That's unheard of in a black movie, and even more so in a dance movie. Everyone really came together to make something special and that magic resonated throughout the cosmos.

That's when the phone calls started. I was getting phone calls left to right from people that I looked up to, and it started getting weird. I was such a rookie in that realm and I was just so talent-focused that I missed the game in which I was now playing in. I landed on Plymouth Rock and everybody in my life got uncomfortable about it.

Way before social media was a big thing and everyone was judged by the numbers they pull, this showed me that it truly doesn't matter how MANY eyes are on something – it matters WHOSE eyes are on something. This can literally be applied in any career field or aspect in life in general, too.

Just keep going. You never know who's watching.

Receiving an award

8

A TEENAGE DREAM

I kind of glossed over the fact that I had a whole entire wife before I could even legally buy alcohol. With the life I've lived, small details like that get lost along the way.

Touring with *STOMP* from the age of 17 to 19 was amazing. I got to see the entire world and get paid to do what I love, but when I got home, it was right back to reality. I only had around $17,000 saved from the tour, and just six months into being back in California, that money was gone. I had to go live with my mom again, and she had one cardinal-rule: church is every Sunday. There were no negotiations on that.

We were raised very Pentecostal, and that's a really strict religion. I had a healthy fear of Hell, but I didn't really know God. I just knew that I didn't want to go to Hell, so I did what was asked of me. This first meant cutting my dreads upon my return to the church because "God didn't like that." I was 19 and I didn't have the relationship with God that I have now, so I was easily manipulated by what I had been indoctrinated into.

Young Columbus

This was only the first thing, though. Not long after, the pastor's daughter tells me, "I'm going to set you up with Brandi." Then they took it a step further.

"You need to be married! You can't be out here a single man. That's just not of God."

So I went and I got married. It was truly an unofficial arranged marriage, and Brandi was all for it. In hindsight,

I honestly think she was the one pushing for it. This STILL wasn't enough, though.

I had yet to fulfill my dream of acting on the biggest level yet, but I was successful! However, my success was only in the secular world. Not only did that mean almost nothing to my church, but it was actually wrong to them. They made me feel really and truly horrible about dancing, doing music, acting; all of these things that I loved. They weren't "of God," so they actually convinced me to quit the business. I really quit. I remember it like it was yesterday, out to dinner with Brandi, her father Anthony and her stepmother Laura.

Anthony was grilling me about my plans, wanting me to go to college and get a "real" job, which to him was basically only a corporate 9-5. And I told them I wanted to be a movie star, I wanted to act, produce music, create art! He chuckled at me and looked to Laura who rolled her eyes in disgust before telling me I needed to get a grip on reality.

"Do you know how unlikely it is that you're going to be this huge movie star or make it as a big-time producer? I need you to get your head out of the clouds and get real, Columbus."

And in the moment, even though I believed whole heartedly in my talents and abilities, I made an internal agreement with his notion. If you've read the book *The Four Agreements* by Don Miguel Ruiz, he writes about the power of the tongue and its ability to be used as either black magic or white magic. And I think unbeknownst to anyone at the table – myself included at the time – I let that black magic settle into my spirit and agreed!

In the blink of an eye, I went from a single dancer/actor/musician with dreads to a married man with a fade who produces gospel music, runs a youth choir and works in sales in an office at Bally's Total Fitness. I was 19, and I married a 24-year-old virgin. I've said this before and I will say it again: my life can truly compete with the script of any film or show that I've been on.

Brandi's parents put down a large sum of money for the wedding, and they paid for the honeymoon in Hawaii too. Everybody was for this, and all I could do was go along for the ride at that point. I wanted to be right in God's eyes.

I remember the day of the wedding so vividly. It was this huge deal and they put on a big ass display with the groomsmen and bridesmaids, and such a beautiful setup on the beach. It was straight out of a fairytale! If only I had actually wanted that.

I took myself to the hotel bar before the ceremony started, and I ran into my pastor.

"You ready for this?" he asked me.

"I don't want to get married," I finally admitted out loud. I braced myself for his response because I knew he wouldn't agree with me, but I had to let it out. I'd been internalizing these feelings and hadn't even said admitted out loud to myself that I was feeling like that, but I couldn't hold it in any longer. His response truly surprised me, though.

"If you don't want to get married, don't do it."

He didn't even finish his complete sentence before tears started streaming down my face. Reality hit me like a ton of bricks when I said it out loud, and I knew that my life as I knew it was about to completely change unless I made an extremely hard decision, one that would also affect my life negatively. I was damned if I did and damned if I didn't.

"But her dad spent all this money and everyone at the church is going to hate me!" I wanted so badly to be liked and not ridiculed. I wanted to be a good saved young man, but cared more about pleasing people than God.

And it wasn't just that. My mom was so active at the church. It was her entire life, and I knew that if I backed out now, it would create a world of drama for her. I couldn't do that to her. Once again, I was worried about everyone else's feelings.

So, I got married. And the honeymoon was just as bad as I thought it would be. We were in a beautiful place like Hawaii, but I didn't want to touch her. I wouldn't sleep with her at all.

On the flight back to Los Angeles, I had a dream that I was doing a movie. It was so real and so vivid, and in that dream, I told Brandi that I needed to get back into acting. It felt so freeing to say that. The happiness and true sense of self I got from doing what I love flooded back to me immediately. When I woke up, I knew that I couldn't keep deferring the inevitable. I wasn't going to continue walking around like a shell of my former self for another day.

"I have to get back to doing what I love," I said as soon as I opened my eyes.

Naturally she freaked out, wondering how we were going to live. I honestly didn't know and I told her that, but I really didn't care. The very next day I walked into Bally's and I quit. She got a job with a temp agency eventually, and I just got back to my grind. I'd sit at home until like noon every day, and then I would drive from Anaheim to Van Nuys to my boy's studio. I'd be in the studio all night and teaching classes. I was so hungry! By this point we'd consummated our marriage, and before I knew it, she was two months pregnant.

It was then that I landed the gig with Brit, and it was all downhill from there...or uphill depending on your vantage point! Now that I was busier than I'd ever been, I was no longer in church every Sunday like I used to be. As the weeks passed, I was separating further from their ideologies, and the idea of our "marriage" became less and less important to me...to the point that I just moved on all together. She hadn't, though.

While I was working, dating other people and trying to make my dreams a reality, she was just lying to our church and to our parents saying that I was "busy," so this made for some really awkward moments when the tabloids started hitting. We were already separated at this point and I had moved on with Stephanie, but technically, we were still legally married.

To me, that was just a small detail. The divorce was going to happen when I had time to sit down and deal with it, and in the interim, I hoped we could behave like adults and live our separate lives. Unfortunately, that was not her game plan. Her trying to save face for the church folks ended up biting her in the ass in the end, and of course I had to take a hit for that also...even though I was being a man about mine and keeping it completely transparent with her from jump.

When I popped up on the cover of *U.S. Weekly* with Britney Spears looking like we were kissing, the shit hit the fan. She hadn't told a soul that we were separating and getting a divorce, so all of the drama I wanted to avoid in the first place came back tenfold. The entire church thought I was an adulterer, and not only was I single and free to do what I wanted, but I wasn't even doing what they were condemning me for! Brit and I were just going in for a hug!

Ultimately, Brandi didn't sign the divorce papers for months and months until after I was fired from Britney's team. And down the line when I was trying to marry my next wife, I had to wait until Brandi finally signed. Eventually, my mom convinced her to sign the divorce papers. She signed May 2004 and then I married *that girl* July 5, 2005.

As I look back on things now, maybe God was trying to save me from the second marriage by giving me this stubborn woman for my first one. Sometimes we need to pay attention to the signs! But to my credit, how was I to know that I was about to marry the Devil in a white dress?

I try to reflect on every negative experience in my life and figure out what the lesson was, and with this one, I couldn't figure it out for a long time. I was angry that despite me being honest with her and doing things "the right way," it still came back to bite me in the end. But ultimately, I realized that you have to follow your gut and do what you know is best for you, not what will please the people around you.

I knew that I didn't want to be married, I knew that I didn't want to give up my passions and not pursue my dreams; but I chose to do those things to please people who in the end didn't even matter to me. Who gives a rat's ass what random folks at church think? Are they paying my bills or even laying their head next to me at night?

To quote *1 Corinthians 2:11*, "For who knows a person's thoughts except the spirit of that person, which is in him?

So also no one comprehends the thoughts of God except the Spirit of God." At the end of the day, you need to do what's best for you.

Living for everyone else will only make you lose yourself in the process.

9

THAT GIRL

F ollowing the blackball that I was facing from Britney, I really couldn't get a job anywhere. It was to the point that I couldn't even go to an open audition! Janet Jackson was having an open call, and her choreographer, Gil, had called my agency to tell them personally that I was not allowed to come. I had the "he fucks artists" stigma attached to my name and it reeked.

This was definitely one of my lower points. I couldn't book a job during this time to save my life, and all of the people that I thought I was cool with wanted nothing to do with me. I was still with Bloc Agency, but they really couldn't get me in anywhere. It was wild.

Bloc had a party one night, so I stepped out for the evening to have some fun. I didn't really know what to expect, considering that the room would be full of the same people who haven't really been fucking with me, but I needed a night out. Steph wasn't with me anymore either, so I really just needed to be around some better energy.

As I expected, the party was nothing but diva dancers, and no one came up to me to speak to me...except *her*. We'd previously met years back during the American Music Awards and she remembered me from that. She was the only one who came up to me to ask if I was okay.

"I've been seeing the headlines," she said. "Are you good?"

I told her the whole story in the middle of the party, and we just clicked. We left that night and talked some more, and we just never stopped talking. Talking quickly turned into dating and dating quickly turned into moving into an apartment together with four other people. *That girl* was an original Pussycat Doll and she brought two more Pussycat Dolls with her, and I had my two boys, Paul and Kenny. Now the six of us were living in this small Mexican casita in the middle of Burbank, and this was my new life.

As one would imagine in any small home with that amount of people, we were all miserable as fuck. I was even more depressed because I was out of the dance game, but it was even deeper than that. I was "in love," but yet I wasn't feeling any more whole than before, like I thought love was supposed to make me feel.

I was empty.

There was one specific morning that I remember distinctly. *That girl* was frantically running around because she had an audition for some small co-starring role, but you'd think she was up for the lead in a major film with the way that she was fucking behaving. Admittedly, I was a bit of an actor snob because I'd been acting my entire life, and I'd had my own issues with the game because of the circumstances I was facing. I actually was still with my childhood agent, Cindy Osbrink, but I hadn't even contacted her in over a year and a half because I'd branched so far out on the choreography route.

I agreed to help *that girl*, who was still frantically running around and panicking. This is what it looks like for amateurs when they're getting ready for auditions.

She handed me the pages she'd printed out, and I quickly glanced over them as I told her to calm down. I handed the pages back to her and started spitting the lines at her, but instead of spitting them back at me, she just gave me a confused and frustrated look.

"How the hell do you know these lines?" she asked, exasperated.

"I just read it," I replied with a hint of an attitude. "You saw me read it."

"I've been studying this for a week and a half!" she

said with an incredulous sigh. "You should be an actor, Columbus!"

What she didn't know was that I *was* an actor. I'd been an actor since I was a child. I like to keep a few tools in the bag at all times; not everyone needs to know everything that I'm capable of, and this was one of those things that I had never let her in on. I ended up telling her about my background, and she decided to just skip her audition. She was too nervous, and I only made it worse by showing her an example of someone who is actually prepared and ready for it.

Later that day, allegedly "impressed" with how effortlessly I remembered the lines she'd been struggling with, *that girl* convinced me to call my agent—despite the fact that I really was reluctant to just pop up a year and a half later, acting like shit was sweet. I knew they were going to chew my ear off when I called, but at the same time, what did I really have to lose? I was barely working, and at least the acting world was an industry I wasn't blackballed from.

I looked at my phone for a minute and decided to just bite the fucking bullet. I hit "call" on Cindy's agency's number, and they answered right away.

"Can I speak to Cindy, please?"

"Who's calling?"

"It's Columbus Short.

After a brief pause, Cindy and her team get on the

phone, and all I heard was, "Well, well, well, Mr. Short!" I had to convince them that I was really ready, and they believed me. I locked in a meeting for the very next morning, and *that girl* was shocked.

"Did you just call an agent and get a meeting...just like that?"

While she was actually impressed at how I could remember those lines and spit them back at her, that wasn't really why she convinced me to call Cindy. I could tell that she thought I was bullshitting before I called them and challenged me to do so because she thought she'd be able to call my bluff. Now I was sitting there with a full meeting on the calendar, and despite the supportive girlfriend role she was attempting to play, I could see the jealousy starting to fester.

At the meeting the next day, Cindy agrees to re-sign me — but there are some terms and conditions. I have six months of "probation," and if I even so much as show up late to an audition, I'm done. And choreography? That's out. They don't want to hear a single word about it.

The very next day, I had an audition. In three days, I went from not knowing what my next move was, to having an agent and being sent out on auditions already. And just like that, I booked the gig, and now Debbie Allen was directing me as part of the Boyz N Motion on *That's So Raven*.

That's So Raven Cast

The Boyz N Motion were a fake boyband, so it was actually really cool that despite the hard "no choreography" rule Cindy had hit me with, I still got to dance and even sing in the role. I played "Trey" alongside Michael Copon as my bandmate Ricky and Ryan Hansen as J.J.J. (Real ones know the deal with that third J.) It was also pretty ironic that the premise in our debut episode was that we met Raven when we came to San Francisco to shoot a music video—the very same city I got my start in with *STOMP* years earlier.

It wasn't the biggest role of my career, but it was the push that I needed to get me back into the acting world and a simultaneous reminder that when you stop procrastinating on your dreams and really put your mind to it, life has a funny way of working out. By the way, I heard that Anneliese van der Pol (Chelsea on the show) said she'd love to see the gang back together when the *Raven's Home* reboot premiered a couple years back. We may need to do that one time for the culture.

Anyway, I should have known then that me and *that girl* were embarking on the beginning of the end. The writing was on the wall, but I didn't think the jealousy would lead to that fateful day on the set of *Scandal* years later, though. But I get it. I started booking gigs back to back to back, while *that girl* was struggling to even get auditions. *That's So Raven* wanted to keep bringing me back, then I did a big episode of *ER,* then I booked a big guest-starring role on *Judging Amy*.

My career was taking off, and *that girl* just had to go along for the ride. And man, what a ride it would be.

10

BEYONCÉ, TAKE MY WIFE

I have been through a lot and I've seen a lot, and I can be the first to admit that it has made me a difficult person to deal with at times, especially in my earlier days. In every situation that I go through, I like to sit back and reflect and really try to figure out not only the core of the problem, but more importantly what I did to contribute to it. It always takes two to tango.

With *that girl* having been a significant, if not the greatest, source of my problems during the peak of my career, I have racked my brain many a night trying to figure out how the hell we got to the place that we did. I can confidently say it was not all me.

So, why do I think she slept with my friend on the set of *Scandal* and all of the other wild, dark and perverse things she's done? There are a handful of things, but it's really spiritual and it's deep.

When *that girl* and I met, she was, as the kids say, "booked and busy." Remember, this was a time when I was blackballed and barely working at all, while she was a popular dancer and video girl. She was already deep in the game in the dance world, and it was even starting to open up doors where she was dabbling in Hollywood here and there as well and rubbing elbows with celebrities daily. Then I enter the picture.

There was an interesting power dynamic in the beginning that quickly shifted, and I think that played a huge role. I was out of work and she found this broken lamb or this broken deer that she could love and care for, but she didn't know that she'd actually found a baby gorilla. She found a cute, cuddly baby beast and she was like, "I'm going to take care of this gorilla and I'm going to love this gorilla!"

And she did! She stepped right in on some, "*WE* got this. You're going to get back on your choreography shit in a major way soon." Was it really for me or was it self-serving, though? I don't know. I think everyone has something in them where they want to be needed and loved, right? Here she found this hurt, talented person and maybe in her mind it was like, "I'm going to hold him down and help him get on his feet, and he's going to love and appreciate me for all that I've done, and we can be a power couple." And I really get it, and I really appreciate that she wanted to help, I just don't think she was mentally prepared for that power shift.

I ended up strong-arming my way back into the dance industry in a major way and then went on to become this huge actor, and I really don't think she knew how to handle that. *That girl* wanted to break away from the mayhem of the music business – because it can really take its toll on you – and so the corners and catacombs and the places she's been I really had no idea of. I had no way of knowing exactly what she'd seen before me. Then I enter her life and we fall in love and all of these things, and by that time, she was slowly trying to make her exit from that part of the game while I just kicked in the door.

I think when I blew up and I was thrust into this fast-paced Hollywood life, she kind of got left behind. And it was definitely not intentional on my part, but I think it was more of a natural shift. She wanted to be where I was, in those rooms, getting those roles. She wanted to be a movie star, while this person she'd met at the bottom of his career was actually surpassing her now and realizing her own dream. Then you have to factor in the idea that I was now hanging around the people that she came up with in her dance days because the game was shifting to a place where music and Hollywood were merging. At this point she'd already been feeling the power shift, but now the paranoia sets in like, "What is he doing with those women?" She knew how a lot of people move in the game, and she started to get suspicious and worry that I was doing things that I wasn't even doing!

I was one hundred thousand percent faithful to *that girl* for the first five years of our marriage. (Spare me on the, "Okay but what about the *whole* marriage?" commentary. You've seen how shit went down.) And please note: we were only really, truly together for seven years and married for ten. Those final years I went wild was only because it was coming to me that she was out there doing her own thing. And I can admit that I didn't have the time or mental space to really deal with those things head-on, so I chose to act out in my own way. I'm not proud of that and I know that's one of the many reasons that my life went as left as it did, but again, it takes two to tango.

Once everything collided, it all hit the fan. I was now on the hottest show on television and we all know how that went, and it goes back to when she came back from touring with Beyoncé on the *I Am...* tour. She was different. Period.

Beyonce and I

It was me, Columbus, who personally asked Bey to take *that girl* on tour. I did that for *her*! Bey had called me and had me come up to a dance studio looking to work with me. She'd just gotten married to Jay at that point, and knew what tour life was like, so when I suggested she hire *that girl*, she was a little concerned.

"Columbus, seriously. You know what goes on out there," Bey told me. "Are you sure you want to send her out on the road?"

I was beyond sure. I fully knew what I could be up against, but I didn't care at that point. She was stressing me out to the max at home and I needed a break! A real break! Again, Bey asked if I was sure and without hesitation I responded, "Take her!"

In hindsight, I regret it because that's what changed everything. Okay, I won't say that I regret it now because it made me who I am today, but in those moments when I was dealing with her shit when she returned from tour, I wished I had never done that. I remember sitting and thinking how different things could be if I just never told Beyoncé to take her...I may in hindsight have ended up dead now that I think about it!

It was 2009 that things started getting really bad, and it was crazy because at the same time, I was having more fun in my career and my social life than I'd ever had. I had an amazing assistant who was helping me take care of my son from my first marriage, I was working on my album, I had a healthy social life; life was great! But slowly but surely, the foundation started to give way.

There is one particular day that sticks out in my mind as a tangible example of the way that shit was going downhill. I had a showcase for Def Jam lined up that night, and we'd already done one at SIR Studios in Hollywood. It had gone pretty well, and now it was time for round two. Beyoncé happened to be in town for this one, and because of that, my wife and her friends were in town too. *That girl* came in to see my rehearsal earlier that day with one of her homegirls who danced on Bey's tour, Ashley, and she saw that I had two dancers that she hated. One of them was her ex-best friend and the other was one of my best friends. She completely shut down the rehearsal. Keep in mind that I have a full band and everything, and *that girl* just shut it down and pulled me off stage right then and there.

"Those girls got to go."

"Karla and Brandy? Are you for real" I asked, fully exasperated because I was tired of her shit. "Come on, man! We've been rehearsing for two weeks!"

Of course, that didn't matter to her.

"We'll learn it right now." She always had an answer for everything. "Me and Ashley are here; we'll put on the clothes and we'll do it right now."

So what does she do? She literally fires those two dancers and replaces them with her and her homegirl one hour before my showcase. I'll give them credit: they did actually learn it, but by then it didn't matter. It just wasn't as clean as we'd had it before and my energy was all the way fucked up. My whole vibe was off!

And that is just one of the examples of the kinds of moments I was dealing with when it came to her during and after Beyoncé. She'd come in town, disrupt my life with her confusion and foolishness, and then go back on the road, leaving me out here to deal with the mess she made.

The Losers

A few months later, I went to Puerto Rico to shoot this movie called *The Losers*. The director, Sylvain White, had worked with me on *Stomp the Yard* and asked how I'd feel about my wife playing my wife in the movie. I thought it was perfect! She'd have a good emotional connection to it, and it would give her a chance to really get her foot in the door. The thing was, she was still out with Bey, so she'd have to make a decision about whether she wants to stay there or come and work with me.

I pitched it to her and she was so with it! She told me that she was quitting Beyoncé and that she was coming to do this role in Puerto Rico. I found out later that she didn't quit, she'd already been fired because she was verbally abusing everybody! *That girl* was on some high horse, pulling the whole, "Do you know who I am? I'm Columbus Short's wife!" not wanting to carry luggage and all that. Crazy.

She did that wild high horse act another time too when I'd gotten her a movie at Sony called *Burlesque* a month after *The Losers*! It became her M.O. I started getting calls from studio execs like, "Yo, you've got to get your wife under control. She's down here tripping talking to people crazy, parking in places that aren't hers!"

She was parking where I parked when I'd work, but she was there as a dancer! You've got to park in the parking structure. She even cursed out Christina fucking Aguilera in front of the entire set because she felt that Christina had talked to her homegirl crazy. And of course, Christina shut down production and it was an entire nightmare. I'm at home chilling watching golf and I'm getting blown up from Sony.

"Columbus get your fucking ass down here right now! Get your ass down here right now!" Clint Culpepper was screaming at me. Yes, the President of the entire company.

Clint Culpepper and I

When I got down there it was mayhem! Production was shut down and Clint was fucking pissed!

"I'm so sick of your shit, Columbus! You need to get your wife under control!" Clint screamed. "She either needs to go apologize to Christina right now or she's fired and you're never working at this studio again!"

So I have to go have this moment with her, and of course she apologizes. And of course we're back in the same cycle.

I don't want to put her business out there, but then again, I have to for full scope of who this person was. Through these rough periods from the Bey tour in 2009 through 2010 – when the two movies wrapped and eventually were released – she was not only in relationships with other dudes but other women on the side too. I was hearing through the grapevine that she had full-blown girlfriends and all of these things and it was just a lot of drifting apart and messiness going on in that time period, on both of our parts.

Now *Scandal* got picked up in 2011, and that year was great for me because it was my first season on the show and I was coaching my son's football team. It was really cool because *Scandal* was on board with me coaching, and they'd let me wrap by 5 p.m. to be in Chatsworth by 6 p.m. to coach. It was just a good time in my life – and I coached my son to championship football! It was when season two came around that *Scandal* was really blowing up and I could see the more the show was getting bigger, it was getting darker on the other side.

As for filming *The Losers*, it was amazing. It was me, Idris Elba, Zoe Saldana and Chris Evans, and Zoe had just recently played my sister in a movie I'd done called *Death at a Funeral*, so it was just serendipitous that we booked this movie together. And when I say "just recently," I mean we wrapped *Death at a Funeral* on a Friday and we were in Puerto Rico by the following Monday. And though my wife landed the role, she didn't appear in Puerto Rico until later because her part was significantly smaller.

Zoe Saldana and I

The movie was dope because it was the adaptation of the *Vertigo* comic books, so it was a lot of really cool action scenes that we got to do. My character Pooch was married to *that girl*'s character Jolene, and after Pooch gets shot in both of his legs at the end, the crew helps him get to the hospital to be there for Jolene giving birth to their son.

Puerto Rico was truly life-changing. We were shooting in the jungle sweating like pigs, but then at night we called ourselves Team Xtreme – me, Idris, Zoe and Chris - because we would work 15 hours and then party all night. And we each had our very own three-story, four-bedroom house. We were out there living like kings and queens.

Despite the seemingly tortuous schedule we were putting ourselves through by capping off our long days with even longer nights, we were making great work. (I can't say the constant partying wasn't screwing up my punctuality, though.) It was one of the most fun productions I've ever been a part of. For the three months we were there, I had the time of my life and I even learned Spanish. It was truly amazing, until *that girl* came down and of course killed all joy that I'd created. Thankfully she wasn't in Puerto Rico with us that long, but it was long enough to leave her mark of destruction once again.

I know we were going through a lot, but I still loved her and I was trying to make it work. And when we both got back to L.A., she claimed she really did want to work on our marriage, but she was so see-through. Why did she want to work on it all of a sudden? Because I'd gotten a new gig.

We were technically separated whenever I wasn't working, which I guess is kind of ironic considering she and I connected when I wasn't working. She was out when I shot the pilot for *Scandal*, but a few months later when it got picked up, my phone was lighting up with a text from her.

"Congratulations on the show! I want to see you today."

Mike Tyson and I on the golf course for a celebrity tourney

I didn't even know the show got picked up because I was on the golf course. It was a stupid cycle I kept spinning myself in, and I think that contributed to everything. I hated fighting with her, so I think that contributed to a lot of the reasons why I would drink back then, which very quickly moved into using cocaine and molly and just doing dumb shit. It's like, for what? And that's the contributing factor: I was so uncomfortable in my life and in my relationship, so I soothed my discomfort with toxic devices.

When you're happy at home, you can be at peace. If you're battling the world and then you have to go home and battle there too? Forget it! There is no peace. The Bible says there is no peace for the wicked, but I wasn't wicked, just deeply immersed in a wicked world! I was dealing with stuff on so many different levels, that maybe it was making us both wicked. I don't know. Then this sounds wild on both sides, but I didn't know at the time that she was practicing witch craft. Yes, she was a real witch! Go figure! I wish I'd at least known about it. You can't just play around with that and make those decisions on your own in a whole marriage! Things like that really conjured up spirits and dark forces, and when you open up spirits and expose yourself to them, shit really can get cray!

Over the next four years, we stayed together on and off. 2012 was the *Scandal* incident, and she filed for divorce in 2013 and again in 2014. At one point, I moved into this house up in Chatsworth after we'd had a nuclear fallout. The shit was so ugly. There are things I don't even want to discuss. Just know, it was getting really, really bad.

I moved on my own and she had to get a place of her own, and I think that really threw her for a loop. I don't think she thought I was really going to go and get my own house, but I did. My friends and assistants helped me with the move – something she would have done if we were functioning, so that was bittersweet.

I got home from work one night and I was having a little house warming around 11 p.m., when I got a call from the security at the front gate.

"Mr. Short, your wife and daughter are out here."

Come the fuck on! I specifically put her on the 'Do

Not Access' list because every time she would come around, there would be drama. She was always on go-mode, ready to go from 0 to 100 immediately, and the whole point of me getting my own place was to avoid that!

I didn't want drama, so I opted not to get any. I didn't let her in, but then she just sits out there for an entire hour. I couldn't have my daughter sitting in a car at midnight! That's nuts! *That girl* knew exactly what she was doing by bringing our daughter with her. So, I let her in. But I wasn't going to just cave like I would tend to do and as she expected me to. As she was gushing over how nice my house is, I swiftly brought her back down to reality.

"Get some rest," I told her. "I've got to be at work at 6 a.m. so I'm laying it down, and you can't be here when I get back. Period."

Her "whatever" response seemed to me like she actually got it. Great. I went to work and came back feeling good, and yet, lo and behold, her car was still parked in front of my home upon my return. What the fuck?

I walked into my house and all that I could see was a sea of boxes. In the moment, I was thinking that she was just taking the boxes of hers that were in my garage and figuring out what to take back to her place, but no. She had actually unpacked the boxes, hung up her clothes in a closet and organized her shit. She'd taken it upon herself to move into my brand-new house. I don't even know what her game plan was with whatever place she'd gotten for herself since our split.

That girl started hitting me with the whole "I want to work on our relationship" babble, and all I could think about was my daughter. I knew I shouldn't have, but I figured for the sake of my little girl, I'd just deal with this until I could figure a way to get out. I'm sure you can imagine that didn't last very long at all.

About a week into this new arrangement of sorts, I had security telling me this person came in and that person came in, and I was seeing all types of people coming and going on my security cameras. *That girl* was just having anyone and everyone come by MY – not OUR – home and I had to quickly kill that. I told her that was just not how shit was going to work in my house and that she could go if that was how she wanted to operate, and apparently, that didn't put a very good taste in her mouth.

I brought one of my friends, an artist I was working with by the name of Tilly, over to work that night in a studio I had built in the crib – and this particular artist happened to be a woman. Not even an hour into our session, here comes *that girl*.

"Who is this bitch in my motherfucking house?!"

Here we go again.

"First of all, this is not *your* house. And we're in a session right now!"

This is a real session with a real artist, and *that girl* was coming to once again mess up my money. You may have seen the video of her beating up a woman on the internet. Now you have the real story behind that.

I actually had recorded that clip, just as a way to document the shit that I was going through to show someone at some point like, "Look, this is not me! She is doing this!" The fight was so ridiculous and pointless and, in the end, really messed Tilly up. *That girl* was spitting on her, hitting her, calling her every single name in the book! My favorite quote in that whole situation was, "Fucking bitch, get the fuck out of my house!" I'm sorry, *whose* house?

Now personally, I prefer to take my L's in private, and this moment would have definitely been one of them. Unfortunately, Tilly wanted the video to be shared "to show *that girl* is violent and even threatened her life," so it made its way to TMZ. Tilly ended up actually pressing charges on her and allegedly "suffered a concussion, a cervical sprain, multiple contusions, a lumbar sprain and lumbar strain," but I don't know how much of that is accurate. I do know that *that girl* was hit with a battery charge months later, though.

But back to the direct moment: she really had to go after this one. I kicked her out and she was gone for a couple of days, but then it was the same cycle. She came back. I let her back. I am as at fault for all of it as she was.

I came home one night and at that point, I'd been living there only about two weeks. Yes, all of this insanity has happened over the course of 14 fucking days – and it was only about to get crazier. It was nearing midnight and I walked into my kitchen upon arriving back home. Keep in mind, the house is so big that you can't hear when someone comes in the front door unless you're physically right there.

When I walked into the kitchen, I saw my iPad opened just illuminating the room from the island in the middle. There on the screen was an email between *that girl* and her boyfriend. The crazier shit is that I already knew about this nigga, so that wasn't even the bombshell. She'd already admitted he existed to me, but it's what the email said that was the real wild part.

"Don't talk about this over email," his email said. "When can we meet up?"

I'm thinking, "Talk about what?"

"I can't take it anymore," she'd replied. "How do we just get rid of this nigga?"

I seriously read those words, from my wife, on my iPad, in my home. Somehow, I was still eerily calm at that point, and I grabbed the iPad and a bottle of wine and ran upstairs to find her. She was sitting in my bedroom when I walked in.

"Oh my God, you scared me!" she said with a weird, nervous giggle.

"I'm sure I did. Let me ask you something, though," I said as I turned the iPad toward her. "Tell me what this means?"

She grabbed it and looked at it and squinted at it, doing a whole fucking song and dance.

"I don't even remember sending that!"

Wow, that's a really great answer.

"Get your shit and get the fuck out of here. Get the fuck up and get the fuck out."

I was done. Now my calm was starting to leave me, and I was talking shit and pacing around while she was in the closet trying to get her stuff.

"Really?!" I screamed in between chugs of wine. "'How do we get rid of this nigga?'"

I had to go downstairs at that point because I couldn't even look at her, but about 20 minutes later, I hadn't heard any movement. What the hell was she doing?

I ran back upstairs after an extended period of silence, and I found her on the floor of my closet just crying. Save the crocodile tears. That shit wasn't working this time. I. Was. DONE.

"Why the fuck aren't you moving?"

"What do you want me to say, Columbus?"

You know that bottle of wine that was in my hand? It ended up being poured on her head. I'd really reached a breaking point. There wasn't that much left since I'd already downed a lot, but once the last drop was out, I left the closet still screaming, "Get the fuck out of here!" I walked downstairs and finally moments later, I could hear her coming down – but then I heard her open our daughter's door.

Nah, homie.

"You're not doing it like that. You're not taking her!" I yelled at the top of my lungs. "YOU have to get the fuck out, and she's staying here."

"Fuck you!" was the response I got back.

That girl ran off with our daughter and seconds later, I could hear the garage door open. I grabbed a knife from the kitchen and made my way outside. My intention was to use the knife to flatten the tire so she wouldn't be able to drive off with my daughter in the middle of the night. Was it a good plan? Certainly not! But it was all I could think of at the moment.

When I got outside and got behind the truck, I felt like she was going to try to run me over. Of course, that's exactly what she tried to do. She tried to run me over, so I stabbed the tire with one jab and the tire went flat. She had our daughter in her lap at that point because our nanny had the car seat.

"You can't drive with her on your lap!" I'm screaming at her.

She drove off into the night like that and that was the last time I saw our daughter. Retelling that night's events now really are so alarming to me on so many levels. It bothers me to this day that my daughter had to hear and witness all of that. It was truly poor form on behalf of both parties and a moment I would definitely take back and handle differently given the chance.

Two weeks following that fateful night, I was at a point where I was just trying to rebuild my life, despite everything that had happened. I had all of this mess that *that girl* once again left behind, but she couldn't just leave me be. She was now attempting to paint the picture that I had threatened to kill her and kill myself! I knew how full of bullshit that was, so I wasn't really responding – and *Scandal* thankfully knew too. The problem was, they were tired of the headlines. It seemed like every other week I was making the tabloids and the blogs with some shit, and they were over it.

They told me they'd rock with me on this one, but if anything more came out, I would be a wrap.

Naturally, this left me overwhelmed and terrified, because I knew what type of terror *that girl* was capable of. I was losing my mind wondering what else to expect from her. I knew she was going to fight to the bloody end, and one of her favorite weapons was controlling the narrative to make me look like the bad guy. Anything could happen. She had the real grave yard type of love, the type of love that if you're not with them then you can definitely not be with anyone else. I knew I had to watch my back because it was far from over.

I needed a break and to just get away, so I went to Arizona to get my mind right. Right on schedule, that's when the headline came out that I had ransacked my house.

"Columbus Short's Wife: HELP! He Ransacked Our Home!!" was the TMZ headline, to be exact.

According to the report, I broke into MY house over Easter weekend while *that girl* was away, "despite a restraining order barring him from the premises" and I "left a trail of destruction" that included breaking a door off its hinges, ripping off "her" bed sheets, leaving on a bunch of lights (that I pay for...) and making her "fear for her safety" and our daughter's safety.

The thing is, I still have the security footage to prove the facts! It was her and her homegirl throwing my patio furniture all in the pool, slashing things, pouring wine all over the couch. I wasn't about to ruin my own couch that I paid for to spite her. What sense would that make? Did you ever see a picture of a beat-up face or someone being choked? No, because that didn't happen! She just ran for her life and she knew that it was over so the best thing to do was flop me.

Shortly after, I had to go to Barbados for a charity event that had been on my calendar for nearly a year. But as soon as I landed for the layover in Miami, I got a call from my lawyer telling me *that girl* had just called an emergency hearing and I had to be in court the very next day. In Los Angeles.

"I literally can't!" I pleaded with my lawyer. "I'm on my way over to Barbados as we speak and I can't miss this commitment!"

"Well, she just screamed bloody murder and said that you threatened to kill her, so this court date is on," he responded.

It was literally always some bullshit. Always! I asked again if we could just deal with it when I got back, and my lawyer told me that he'd see what he could do. Next thing that I knew, I landed in Barbados to a warrant for my arrest in L.A.

Oh, let me add insult to injury real quick – within those two weeks that she had moved back, *that girl* had ciphered out over $350,000 of cash that was going to get me through the summer and pay my taxes before the next season of *Scandal* was going to start again. She took all of that money and then acted like she was broke. If my lawyer wasn't working pro bono anyway, I wouldn't have even been able to retain a lawyer! I was okay in only that particular scenario, but I no longer had any money to do anything else, with nothing set to come in for months. It was crazy.

I still really want to take ownership of some things, though. There was no way that I was going to make this relationship work because the other party was cheating and being toxic, but where I dropped the ball was what I was doing to myself. When I hurt myself, I ended up hurting other people — mostly girls. I was sleeping with strange women and doing all that shit to fill some stupid insecurity and it was not helping to try and revive our broken relationship. It was a complicated cycle; it was you hurt me and I'm going to hurt you back and then it's just a war of the roses.

One thing to my credit – or maybe my detriment – was that I was always brutally honest. *That girl* didn't have to catch me in anything because I didn't care. I would just say, "Yeah I smashed that chick." I was doing that to hurt her because I was hurt. I was trying to act all tough like I didn't care, but I was feeling like shit. To be honest, every time I cheated – even though I knew she was doing it too – I felt gross. I was just running from the situation.

We were both so reckless at a point that her friends thought we were in an open marriage! That was absolutely not something we'd ever discussed, but I was just out there smashing chicks and I figured at the same time, she was telling people that we were open and that's why so many women she knew ended up in my bed. I guess that would define an open marriage, but when it's not something discussed between the two of you, it leaves a lot of blurred lines.

It was a toxic relationship on both ends, and at the end of the day, it doesn't matter who was doing more "wrong" than the other. We both allowed the cycle to continue over and over and over again, making us both equally at fault for our demise. We both were beating a dead horse for way too long, and we both paid for it in the end.

11

SURVIVING COLUMBUS

Alot of times, things happen in our childhood that we don't realize we're "bad" or affected us in some way until we're older. I was getting with an 18-year-old girl when I was eight, and I really thought that was normal. (Or rather, she was getting with me.) It wasn't until I was in therapy at the same time that *Surviving R. Kelly* was blowing the lid off what R. Kelly was doing that I realized what had happened to me wasn't okay at all.

My mom, she did the best that she could with us. I mean, I think that she did. Maybe it wasn't the best, but she tried to do something. I reflect on so many moments in my life and I know that it was a culmination of so many things that led me down a bad path, but I do believe it really started with my mother. A mom is the first woman that a little boy loves, and the fear of abandonment was unfortunately instilled in me so early that I don't think I ever really shook it off.

My mom was working so much that sometimes it just became too much for her to work and take care of us at a point when I was a child; it was like she was starting to crack. My mom doesn't know how much I knew her then and still do; she was the person I studied every day. I could see that she was about to break down. She said she wasn't going to be able to make the money she needed to make to take care of us.

If one of our neighbors would have called child protective services on us, we would have been in a group home. And it's crazy because that is what my mom did: she worked at group homes with kids that had developmental problems and special needs.

Young Columbus

I will never forget this one particular day where we were leaving a Carl's Jr. (which then became and is *still* a huge trigger for me) and my mom pulled over in the parking lot. My brothers were asleep again and I remember telling my mom that I want to go home. She had gone to the ATM and couldn't get money out because there wasn't any to take, and she came back to the car and looked at me with the most defeated look I'd ever seen in someone.

"Mom? Mommy are you ok?" I said as I grabbed her hand. "Mommy?!"

I'd never seen this before and I was so scared. She put her head on the steering wheel and with tears streaming down her face, she looked at me and said, "I don't know how much longer I'm going to be able to keep you boys."

Imagine hearing that from your mother? That hurt me to the core, and particularly because I thought it was my fault. I thought I caused her to feel this way.

"Please don't give up on us, mom! I promise I'll be a good boy!" I pleaded with her.

You have to also remember, I knew foster care very well because that was her job. I was around that. I knew how bad it was out there. I knew group homes from the developmentally handicapped. I didn't want to be there and I didn't want my brothers to be there.

"I really think I might have to let you go," she said through tears.

"Let me go?!" We went home that night, and after church the next day, she was back to normal – but I never was. I was forever traumatized that she was going to bounce at any moment.

I share that to say that I do believe that affected how I handled all of my relationships moving forward, until I finally started doing the work as an adult to learn my triggers and learn my emotional trauma and its layers so that I could begin to heal. That moment made me love my mother unconditionally because it made me step outside of myself and really see her as a human being with real issues and not just "mom." But at the same time, it taught me that I can't trust her because she was liable to get up and leave at any moment.

Having to feel like that at such a young age is so sad, and I can see why I stayed with *that girl* so long; I didn't want to be abandoned. And that sense of fear I think is what made other inappropriate moments with women seem not only normal, but almost comforting to me for so long.

When I was in grade school, my mother would have her friend's daughter take care of me and my brothers during the summer. My brothers would usually just nap all day or keep to themselves in their room, and our babysitter just watched soap operas the whole time. She wasn't worried about us. Well, let me rephrase that: she wasn't worried about *them*.

There was one night I specifically remember watching her sneak some wine, and shortly afterward, she turned to me and said, "Let's do a scene." I loved acting even then, so she knew exactly how to pull me in. This was it.

She told me that I was going to play the dad, she'd be the mom and for storyline purposes, our kids are asleep. At the time I thought it was so cool, but now that I look back on it, it was really fucking weird; this grown woman was sipping wine with an eight-year-old. (I didn't really like the taste, if you were wondering.)

This was a recurring theme after that night. We would

have this candlelit dinner, and she would take me to the couch and then it was just always, "Do you want to do a scene?" Then it would end in something sexual at the end. Let me remind you all once again, I was eight!

The first time that it happened, I was confused and I was trying to grasp the concept of what was going on. Eventually, though, it just got to the point where I'd be looking for her if she wasn't around. She lived in the hood, so a couple of times I went to their house and it was absolutely that same weird shit – the location didn't change the activities. I guess I kind of suppressed a lot of this, though, because it seemingly didn't affect me for some time.

I went about life without any direct feelings of emotional distress, but when stuff started coming to the surface, I went through this real period of thinking women were terrible. From seeing how my mom is, to be completely honest, and all the way to *that girl*, it took a real toll. It's hard to be a normal human being and understand what love and trust really is when these were your examples to rely on.

I never said anything to my mom about the molestation because I just knew I'd get in trouble. It only happened a few years removed from the moment in that Carl's Jr parking lot, so there wasn't even a level of trust there anyway. I thought it was me who was doing something "bad," but honestly even if I had recognized it was abuse at the time, I still don't think I would have told her. I wasn't that kind of kid; I wasn't a snitch. Some kids want to tell on everybody, but I was really the opposite.

I felt like no matter what I said, I was an equal partici- pant and it wouldn't just be her getting in trouble; it would be me getting in trouble too. So, it kept going on and then we moved and it just...stopped. It was a weird year and a half or so of my life, but the overexposure left its mark on me. It really created this infatuation with older girls that would go on to last a really long time. It's crazy how these experiences can do that.

In hindsight, I wish I would have said something because now I look at the fact that I didn't as cowardly. I've never seen that woman ever again but I've forgiven her, because for her to have been doing that, someone must have touched her! For her to feel comfortable, she was probably doing something that was done to her. At 18, I was looking at 30-year-old women, so I will never get what she got out of touching a little kid.

I pray for her and I truly forgive her. I honestly hope that she's gotten the help that she so desperately needed since then. I know that hurt people hurt people. It wasn't okay, but she got it from somewhere else and when that kind of devious behavior starts, that spirit takes on a life of its own. It spreads like cancer and it can affect so many lives.

One person's mental illness can hurt so many others,

and that's why I'm so hyper-protective over my kids and really, just kids in general. I keep a keen eye on weirdos at the park, I question who's at the playground without a kid. I don't like being that type of person because quite honestly, it's exhausting, but it's who I am now.

When my wife and I were watching the R. Kelly documentary, it was just so deeply triggering. That was the first time that I told my wife about what happened to me. She said that so much made sense after that, from how protective I am with the kids to how I get awkward at times with affection. Sometimes I just don't like being touched or rubbed or caressed, even in a loving way; it tends to randomly freak me out, and it's weird. And those are the side effects of going through that kind of stuff.

And that wasn't even the only time that some shit went down with an older woman at a young age.

One summer, my teenaged stepsister came into town with my little brother's dad. It was just a random night that we were all in the house and she got on me! She was sucking on my body and she wound up giving me like three or four hickies. The next day my mom saw me and immediately questioned, "What's that on your neck?"

"*Such and such* was sucking on my neck and it was ticklish!"

I was laughing like it was funny, but let me tell you – my mom found absolutely NOTHING funny about it. She went ballistic and kicked my stepsister out, her father went ballistic – it was a whole thing. And here I was just so cool and casual about the entire ordeal, because of course I was just way too oversexualized way too soon.

It's crazy because when I was in junior high, all of my friends were girl crazy – as they should have been. At like 13, 14, 15, they were all girl crazy and I just...didn't care. It was really like nothing to me. I'd already did it, I'd already lived what they would fantasize about from their twin beds at night while looking at a poster of Carmen Electra hanging on the wall. They wouldn't believe me and I would brag about the fact that she was older than me, but it wasn't really something to brag about. It wasn't cool.

Even when I toured with *STOMP*, I was 17 and traveling the world telling people in some bars in Korea that I was 18. I'd be in different countries throughout Europe telling women who were over 25 that I was 21. It was just so normal to me.

One day on the tour, we were at the bar of some hotel in Phoenix that was having a teacher's convention. The entire hotel was crawling with women who were all in their early to mid 30s. Then enter this 17-year-old kid, pretending to be 21, enjoying a drink at the bar like I was an adult. And I didn't just look the part, I knew how to act the part as well. I knew how to chop it up with folks and how to really act like a grown man, but at the end of the day and at the core of it, I was still just a kid. You can put lipstick on a pig but it's still a pig, isn't it?

I was cracking jokes with three women who had ended up at the bar at one point, and a few drinks later, I was upstairs in a room with all of them. Yep, it was going down. These women were in their 30s and I wouldn't be surprised if one of them was pushing 40 – but that didn't matter to me. I was trying to push something else.

We ended up having a damn good time and once it was all over, we headed back to where it all started. And guess who was there waiting for one of us? The husband of one of the women. And she went right to him like her mouth wasn't just on my thang upstairs 20 minutes earlier. Sorry, homie – the game is the game.

With my current wife, it took us a long time to get to the right place because I had stopped believing in love. I really had lost faith in humanity in general. I had a really negative outlook on human beings because I'd developed this mindset that everybody was shady and that no one was going to change and so what's the point. But through work and self-development and reflection and all of those important things, you find that you have to trust somebody and once I started to trust a little bit, I kept on a little more and little more. You get to see that there are good people and the woman that I love now is a good woman.

I can't clump all women into a category of shade; it

would be unfair because it wouldn't be true. It's crazy to see that the things you suppress and what you think you forgot about are actually always still there until you deal with them head-on. And if you don't, they can manifest themselves in very unorthodox and sometimes inappropriate and damaging ways.

I think that getting down to the epicenter or the cause of what that may be is very important for people to get past whatever the issue is. If you don't know that it's there, you'll never deal with it. It's a simple concept, really, it's just hard to execute. That's why it's important to get to roll your sleeves up, dig down deep and ask yourself, "Why am I feeling like this every time this is happening?"

For example, I'm hyper-protective of my son around both sexes. No one is going to be kissing on my son — I don't play that. I'm not just leaving my kid with anybody, even if there will be more kids there. There are kids that molest kids. You'll have an 8 or 9-year-old who's overexposed to sexuality and they'll do to a 4 or 5-year-old what they saw their older brother do to someone. That type of stuff is what I'm hypersensitive to. I thank God that my issues didn't manifest in any other way, and instead gave me an infatuation with older women and later a distrust of women. Obviously, none of these scenarios are ideal, but if I had to pick a poison, that would be it.

My mom used to say for years to me, and I didn't

know why, "Your body is your own; don't let anyone touch your body." Finally, when I was 19, she told me that she and her siblings were molested by a neighbor when they were young, so that explained a lot about why my mom had all these weird triggers and things. That's something that always resonated with me.

There was a point in my young adulthood that I felt like I wanted to reclaim the childhood that I never had. I had a lot of repressed things. I was scared of everything because of repression from the church, and not to go back to the overexposure to sexuality, but there are a lot of people in the church like the preacher's kid and preacher's daughters that have high levels of promiscuous behaviors. They're more sexualized because they're told from a young age that they can't do this and they can't do that, so it's that rebellion.

I do think there was a point where I was trying to reclaim my childhood, but not reclaim in a cognizant, thought-out way. I think it was more like, "Man, I don't have to do that. I've been taking care of everybody else and I need to take care of me!"

The issue was that I didn't know how to take care of me because I'd been taking care of everybody else. I didn't understand love. Through therapy, self-reflection and finally having the right woman by my side, I'm so happy to say that that's no longer the case. I ended the generational trauma with me.

Presenting an award

12

THE GAME

I've consistently seen the same pattern repeat itself over and over in my life — a bunch of nothing turns into a bunch of everything in the blink of an eye. In the early stages of getting with *that girl,* I went from not working at all, to suddenly being up for three movies at once! I think I can credit my first-born child Jalen, who was a toddler at the time, to the reason that I was so razor-focused. I would actually take him on auditions with me and just put him on the couch, and I really think I was booking some of my gigs because of him. People were so impressed at how well-behaved my little man was.

When I say I was up for three movies, I'm talking about being on the short list. I was auditioning with Steve Pink at Universal for *Accepted.* I was up for a movie called

Jellybean at Warner Bros., which would go on to be the movie we know as *ATL*. I was up for a movie called *Invincible* with Mark Wahlberg. I knew in my heart that I was about to land one of them, and I felt so ready for that next phase in my career. This is the moment that actors work for. Just one of these roles need to connect, and I'd be out of there. And I knew I had it in the bag.

First up was a call from the people at *Invincible*. "We're going to go another way."

That's totally fine. I have *Jellybean* and *Accepted* in the pipeline. One of the two is going to be the one. God got this.

I get the call from Warner about *Jellybean*. "We're going to go with Jackie Long."

DAMN! I had actually been up for T.I.'s role initially, but they ended up testing me for Esquire and narrowed it down to me and Jackie. But Jackie is my boy, so I was happy that if it had to go to someone other than me, it was him. Now it was down to me and Edwin Hodge for *Accepted*....and I didn't get that either. I was up for three fucking roles, testing in front of producers, and I got nothing. Zero.

Depression set in, and with that, my poor decision-making set in too. I was in a constant state of being broken; I never really healed from my childhood. I didn't really understand my feelings at that point, and like a drug, I was using what I thought was love to mask what was going on inside me.

"I'm letting the game dictate my joy and I promised myself I would never do that again," I *told that girl* one July morning. I was so depressed about not booking any of the three roles, and I really thought I had the remedy. "Do you want to get married?" I asked her. "Let's just get married and go live a life and forget the game. Fuck the game. I'm over it."

We got married the next day — July 5, 2005.

The very next morning, I woke up to a call from my agent. Production had already started on *Accepted*, but they needed me on the set right away. I was confused. That's not my movie, why would they need me?

"They just fired Edwin Hodge. It just wasn't working," Cindy told me. "Justin Long didn't like him, the chemistry between him and Jonah wasn't working and Tom said we need to find another guy. Steve Pink wants you to come up to set right now and just throw the football with Tom."

And just like that, the tables turned again. The set ended up being literally right around the corner from my house, and in less than an hour later, I was on the Universal lot throwing the ball with famed director Tom Shadyac. I could tell he was absolutely loving me, and it didn't take long before he was telling me that he wanted me to wait around because Justin was still shooting and he wanted us to improv together to see if it could really work.

After he wrapped, Justin made his way up to base camp and we did a quick improv. Not to brag or anything, but among my many talents, improv ranks high, and so I knew the second that they told me to improv with Justin, I had it. I got the job that day.

The very next day I started filming my first major movie role. Everything really does happen on God's time. We can't plan it, but we can be prepared for it! My character, Hands, was the token black guy in the film, so suffice to say I stuck out. The movie opened up at No. 5 at the U.S. box office and made $38.5 million worldwide on a $23 million budget, so it absolutely did what it needed to do for me.

After that, the ball started rolling faster than I could have imagined. With the $75,000 I got for that movie, I put $40,000 down on a house. A few weeks into shooting, I booked *Save the Last Dance 2*. Filming for *Accepted* wrapped two days after my birthday in September of 2005, and the very next day, I was on a plane to Toronto to film *SLD2*. I'd married *that girl* just two months prior when I was at my wits' end and ready to give up on my dream, and look where I was now.

Ne-Yo and I

SLD2 was a straight-to-DVD movie, but I had the co-starring role. I also loved the fact that much like the Boyz N Motion on *That's So Raven*, it was another opportunity to fuse dance and acting for me. The original *Save the Last Dance* had been an inspiration to me years prior, so it was a bit of a full circle moment to be able to do that one. Ne-Yo had a cameo in it too so we ended up forging a good relationship on set, which was cool because we'd end up working together again way sooner than we would have thought.

Once I finished that movie, I landed back in Los Angeles to a call from my brother Dave Scott, telling me that I HAD to be on the Sony lot the next day. He wanted me to sit down with Clint Culpepper, the President of Sony Screen Gems, because they thought I'd be a great fit for this movie they were developing called *Steppin'*.

"Nah, bro," I told him. "I appreciate you but I'm trying to avoid dance movies at all costs. I want to be taken seriously as an actor. If I keep doing dance movies, they're not going to take me seriously."

I was a real actor; I just so happened to know how to dance really well. And produce. And sing. And play instruments. And write. Plus, I literally had just finished a dance movie and didn't need to do two back-to-back. I'd be typecasted forever!

Somehow Dave convinced me to go, and this included making sure I wore "something tight" to the meeting. I walked into Sony the next day with Timberland boots, True Religion jeans and a beige skintight thermal looking swole, and I sat down in Clint's office with him and Eric Paquette, the SVP at Sony Screen Gems. Man, I was so green. The meeting went great, but it didn't end like I thought it would.

"So yeah, we'll get back to you," Clint told me once our conversation wrapped. "We're doing a nationwide search for this lead, so we'll reach out once we're done with our search."

I looked at him dead in his eyes.

"I challenge you to search the country for a talent that has all the skillsets ready to make this movie, Clint," I said. "Find someone who can dance this movie, who can step the fuck out of this movie and who will act this movie into the ground like I will, Clint. I promise you. I dare you to search the country."

"Get a load of this guy!" he replied laughing, looking over at Eric. "He's either incredibly arrogant, or he's fucking right!"

I knew that I was fucking right. He knew that I was fucking right.

"That's your call," I said as I walked out of the room. Behind me, I overheard him tell Eric, "Did you see the bod on that guy?" Oh, so that's why Dave had me wear this. I knew I had the movie.

I still had to be put through the ringer to make it "fair," so I went and tested against all the guys in Hollywood and ended up earning the job the right way. I got a gig on a major dance movie at a time I was still blackballed from the dance industry! This one wasn't straight-to-DVD like *SLD2*. This was a major motion picture, and I was the lead.

It was a crazy moment — made even more crazy by the fact that it meant I'd be on set with a lot of people who had turned their backs on me in years prior, so I had a decision to make. Did I want to be the kind of man who shits on all of these niggas, or did I want to be the kind of man that encouraged all of these niggas? I decided to be the man that encouraged all of these niggas.

Stomp The Yard

If you were wondering, Sony ended up changing the title from *Steppin'* to *Stomp the Yard* because Channing Tatum's *Step Up* had just dropped with quite a different storyline and they didn't want audiences to confuse the two.

My character, DJ Williams, earned his team in the movie, but I really earned that team in real life. That wasn't just some acting. They couldn't just write that. I created that brotherhood and it matured over six weeks of rehearsal and three months of filming. That happened. I created this brotherhood under everybody's noses, and we really won in the end.

In my first lead role, my little $13 million budget

movie opened at No. 1 in the U.S. box office with $22 million in just the first weekend. Ben Stiller's *Night at the Museum* had been No. 1 for three weekends in a row and we knocked them out! We went on to make $75 million worldwide.

Funny enough, all of that almost didn't happen. I was two seconds away from being fired from *Stomp the Yard* on the very first day and it wasn't even my fault.

Stomp The Yard - Jet Magazine

Clint was of course having trepidations because I was a new name, so the general consensus from everyone was basically like, "He's clearly the most talented and perfect person for the role, but we need to surround him with stars!" This is how Ne-Yo, Chris Brown and Meagan Good were all added. I literally had to beg Meagan to do it.

When we got out to Atlanta, Meagan and I were doing these rehearsals with Sylvain White, the director. Whoever I was in a scene with, we'd rehearse one-on-one with Sylvain. The cast had six weeks of dance rehearsals before we even started shooting, and we were doing dance and step in the morning and then acting in the evening. At this particular point, there were about two weeks until we officially begin filming.

We were really a great team: me, Meagan and Sylvain. The creativity was really going crazy during our rehearsals and we ended up tweaking the script; adding some things and taking off some things. We had all the new additions down flawlessly, and come the first day of filming, I was ready to really show and prove. Not only can this kid act, but he can work with his co-stars to come up with even better choices than was in the script!

We started shooting the first scene where I have no shirt on and I'm riding a tractor, and Meagan forgot literally all of the changes! Instantly! Everything we'd done in rehearsals had went out the window and she reverted right back to the original script! Being that it was day one, of course every single one of the studio execs were on set and they had no idea that we had changed up the scene, so now I looked WILD. They were looking at me thinking that I was the new guy messing Meagan up!

It was really a tough scene to get through, because Meagan was dropping the line changes. In her defense she'd had a late night the night before, and we did rehearse like five different versions of the scene, so I think it all just jumbled together for her. The rougher it got, the more uncomfortable I got. I could see the studio executives sitting at video village shaking their heads. I'm sweating now even recalling it! We eventually got through it, but I knew that it wasn't as good as we both wanted it be. Sure enough, I got a call the very next morning.

"Clint wants to replace you; you were unprepared," the producers told me over the phone. "Come down to the lobby, please."

I started packing my clothes before I even went down. I'd already been thinking it was too good to be true, and there it was.

Sylvain and Will Packer met me in the lobby with serious faces, and my heart was pounding in my throat. I was really hoping Sylvain held me down, because he actually knew that it wasn't me! He was there!

"Clint wants to fire you, but I told Clint that we switched it up," Sylvain said as I walked up. My man! "We're going to work it out, but he wants you on a plane tomorrow."

There was nothing I could do at that point but accept whatever my fate would be, and I told them the same.

When I woke up the next morning, the van was there

to take me to set – not to the airport. I still had a job, and I wasn't going to ask any questions! From that day on, I didn't care what was going on with any other actor or actress. I knew I had to be on my game at all times, especially with me being the rookie in the game. I was playing for keeps. I will always hold both Sylvain and Will in high regard for that day. Saving a career that hadn't even begun yet. BLESSED!

13

AMERIKKKAN BLACK CARD

The road to Hollywood is a program; it's a system. Like most industries, you have a ladder that you have to climb when you come into the game. You probably do a lot of commercials, then you end up getting some guest spots on a network television series. From there you potentially become a series regular, and then finally, you can head on over to the coveted silver screen. That's kind of the journey, although some are lucky enough to fast forward through some of that. They're likely less melanated.

When I was first doing these guest starring roles, I started booking a lot...but all of my roles were gang members. If anybody knows how to play a gang member it's me, right? I was getting all of these gang member roles and it started getting to the point that it was uncomfortable. The dialogue was just so black-heavy, so hood-heavy. There had to be better roles representing our people!

I eventually landed the role in *Accepted* – and the title is so ironic because it was the movie that I was accepted into the game with. But yet, the Unit Production Manager (UPM) on the movie was a racist. I was literally the token black guy in this film. The only other black guy on that set was my stand-in — who ended up being my stand-in on *Scandal*. He was from Kansas City like me, so I was like looking out for him and his career and kind of doing the antithesis of what Denzel Washington would later on end up doing to me.

He wanted to act and he was a writer, so I was helping him out! But I guess he started getting jealous of my success and started feeling like I just wasn't doing enough for him, and that's when he decided that he wanted my wife too.

But hey, that's neither here nor there.

I showed up to work one day literally just five minutes late. And this wasn't five minutes late like I was holding up the cameras – this was the call time that the UPM had given me to get a haircut and makeup. Now, bear in mind that not only did I not need a haircut because my hair was already cut, but I also didn't need makeup. I'd already gone over this with the makeup people and told them that I didn't wear that shit because we were shooting in the middle of August and the foundation they were caking on my face was making me break out.

I've never worn makeup on a movie or anything after that, by the way.

So, this dick of a UPM pulls me to the side as soon as I arrived on set.

"Five minutes late is unacceptable," he hissed in my ear. "I hope you enjoy your 15 minutes; your kind doesn't last long around here, so don't be late again or you won't even be here. Your 15 minutes will be seven."

In my comfort zone

He had some fucking nerve! Mind you, this happened

about a week after Hurricane Katrina had hit in 2005, which meant it was about a week after Kanye West said on national television that President George W. Bush doesn't care about black people. That being said, I was already in this weird space seeing how the people were being treated in NOLA. That was a huge thing for me and then I had to come into work and deal with racist shit from this guy. And that wasn't even the only instance!

On set, they would just do really white boy, stupid, racist things. The black jokes could seem harmless to the next guy, but me coming from being around white people and having to fight the Polar Bears and experiencing racism my whole life at every level — that shit wasn't going to fly with me. All those little quick, funny jokes that these white boys thought were funny, I wasn't sharing the same sentiments. I had to check these fools and I didn't care.

"Justin, you're going to have to stop all of these little racist jokes," I found myself saying to Justin Long way more often than I should have had to.

"C'mon bud! I'm not racist!" was always his reply. "Don't pull the black card on me!"

Now Jonah Hill, that's my boy right there! And Blake Lively is a total sweetheart, but Justin? I'll just say this; racism is real in Hollywood. These white boys are cliquish and unless your name is Denzel Washington, Laurence Fishburne or Don Cheadle, they won't have respect for you. If you're a black man in their age range, they really aren't going to give you any kind of respect.

As the new black guy on the scene, I'm guessing that they all expected me to just take their little jokes and jabs and let them roll, so when I didn't, it became all eyes on me the whole time. They knew like I knew that it doesn't take three PAs to watch me go to the bathroom. And I dealt with that from the first day on set until the last.

It was really trying for me early in my career navigating being a black actor because I knew that I was bigger than the roles that they were being relegated to me. I'm not talking about star power; I'm talking about in real talent. I can act circles around these white boys and I know that, but more importantly – they know that!

That was the first kind of major racism that I dealt with on set, but then there was the unspoken "you should already know that this is how Hollywood is" racism too. And what I mean by that is that Hollywood can break a white boy every week. But with black actors, they might let one in every three years if we're lucky. Thankfully things have started to change in a major way, not only for African American actors but Latinx and Asian performers as well.

At one point, both myself and Denzel Washington were up for this movie called *Safe House*. It ended up being Denzel and Ryan Reynolds in the movie. Why?

Well it had nothing to do with my talent, I can tell you that.

I was at a meeting at DreamWorks with Steven Spielberg and his partner for the film, and they opened with, "Columbus, we love you! You're phenomenal and you killed in *Cadillac Records*."

Okay, okay. So far, so good!

"We would love to put you in *Safe House* but here's the problem..."

I braced myself, but I honestly thought it would be some simple shit that I could easily talk them out of.

"We're going to ride it out because we're out to Denzel and we don't know if we want to go with a younger black and black."

A "younger black and black?" The hell are they talking about?

"What's wrong with that?" I questioned. I had to hear them say it. They wouldn't be so bold, would they?

"You know Columbus, we want to sell internationally, and two black leads just doesn't sell. It feels more like a domestic movie than an international. Denzel has international, but we need that white counterpart to have international as well."

Wow, yep. They said it!

"How am I supposed to go international if you guys don't give me an international movie that's going to be distributed internationally?" A logical question, one would think.

"Well Columbus, your numbers aren't great internationally," they replied. "Your numbers are great domestically, but nobody knows you internationally."

"What do you suggest that I do?" I asked. "How do I get my numbers up internationally if you guys don't give me a movie?"

They ended up telling me to go to television, but at the time, I was completely against doing TV.

"TV right now really builds your star power," they told me. "Build that up and we can't wait to work with you! You just have to build your international side up." Truth is, at the end of the day, everything he said to me was one hundred percent correct. He wasn't being racist; it was sadly being factual. Hard facts to swallow, but in the end...

Scandal would go on to really open doors for me (before my personal drama subsequently closed them), but it was still such an eye-opener into what a person of color is dealing with in Hollywood on a daily basis. Again, I can say things are seriously improving. Cut to now and you have *Black Panther* that's all black and absolutely murdered it at the box office breaking all kinds of records!

NAACP Awards - Scandal

I say all of this to say that coming up in the game, I've experienced racism. I've experienced bullying, betrayals, great heights, great lows and everything in between to get to where I am now to be able to confidently say: I hate Hollywood. I love the screen, I love creating, I love producing, I love writing, I love the creative. I hate to love the game, "the biz." I never wanted to play it, but now I'm playing...and I'm playing fair, but I'm definitely playing for keeps.

I know how it works now and I know what's needed, and all that stuff that hurt my feelings—going through the business with emotions and wearing my heart on my sleeve and hoping that people are friends and people are honest—it helped me learn that people don't care. When you come into this game, you have to have thick skin, you have to be a fighter. You have to be able to get knocked down and get back up a thousand times, no matter what's going on. And that's my message to anybody that does anything!

Coming into a career space, especially in the entertainment industry, you have to have seven layers of skin and a resilience that is almost ignorant. It's a dumb resilience. Like, why would you keep trying to run into this brick wall? Your forehead is bleeding! Don't run into the brick wall anymore! You have to do the same thing over and over again each time expecting a different result, it's clinical insanity!

But I'm the insane one that believes each time that if I run just a little harder one more time, with all my might, I'm going to bust through that wall. And that's kind of been my modus operandi; you don't have to unlock the door, you don't have to open a window. I'm just going to bust through the thing.

I will not be ignored.

14

EXORCISING LITTLE WALTER

I t was 2009 and I was shooting a heist action thriller called *Armored* on the Sony lot. We were working through the strike and so every day, I was pulling in and feeling so bad as I crossed the picket lines. Coming on set with all of the writers outside, I was stuck between two worlds because I wanted to ride with my writers, but at the same time, I was a movie star now and this movie star game is paying the bills. I was also competing against a lot of black actors that were hating that Columbus Short is *the guy* now.

I was the lead in the film and rightfully so because I'd already been racking them up at the box office. It'd been two years since *Stomp the Yard* came out and did numbers, and since then I'd also starred in *This Christmas*, *Quarantine* and *Whiteout*. I was going to be the next Will Smith.

There was only one after Denzel and that was me. "Who's the next one?" It was Columbus Short. Period.

The cast that I was working with was amazing too. It was Matt Dillon, Jean Reno, Milo Ventimiglia, Skeet Ulrich and Laurence Fishburne, who later became not only a mentor but my Uncle Fish. I'll never forget the day he told me I'm the one. Yep, Morpheus told me I was THE ONE!

He came into my trailer one day when we were working; I was in there with Matt, Jean and Milo. Milo and I were sharing a double banger trailer and of course Uncle Fish had his own King Kong joint. (When I say that I mean a humongous trailer with a bed and rooms and all that stuff. You know, big like King Kong.)

"Son, you got a second?" Laurence asked me when he popped into our trailer.

I promptly kicked everyone the fuck out. Of course I had a second! I had every second that Uncle Fish could have needed!

"You know you're the one, right?"

I couldn't believe that he was saying that to me.

"When I was your age, you know what it would have been?" Uncle Fish continued. "Milo would have been the star. He would have been number one on the call sheet. You would have been playing the cop that was being saved by him. You better take this baton and run."

It got even better as he continued.

164

"I just got offered this movie called *Cadillac Records* and I don't want to do it. I don't want to work with them. But you, go get the movie."

The fact that Uncle Fish had told me that was enough, but then I found out that Beyoncé was leading and that it was a blues movie. I'm a musician, I sing – this is perfect. I HAVE to get this movie!

I put a call in to my agents, and they told me that the director, Darnell Martin, wasn't coming to L.A. for auditions; I'd have to go to New York. They also told me that there was an offer out for Omarion to play Little Walter and I was like hell nah! Clearly that offer was because the producer didn't know what she was doing in the movie business. She didn't know much about making real films, she just wanted names. Oh, they also said they were making a choice by Friday. It was Wednesday.

I knew that I wrapped on Thursday that week, so I got a red eye on Thursday night straight after work and flew to New York. When I landed, I called my agents like, "Tell Darnell that I'm in New York today and ask if we could please meet!"

Darnell took the meeting!

She asked that I come to her house as opposed to a studio or office, so I went there, met with her and did the scene. As soon as I finished, she told me, "Oh my God, that was really great! We're going to get back to you."

I didn't even have my dialect coach yet to get my

Southern accent to where it needed to be. I auditioned on my natural instincts and by the time I landed back home, I got the role.

On Monday, Uncle Fish had his assistant send me a number to a dialect coach and said to go see her. Do you think I'm going to question Morpheus? I went to go see her, and that's how I discovered how to break down dialect. It was truly a new level of my game, a next level of tools in my already-extensive belt. I still am so grateful to Laurence Fishburne for doing that for me.

I really felt that this was the role that was going to get me an Oscar, so I was ready to go full out! And I'm competitive. I take my craft very seriously and when I go down into the ground, I want part of my legacy to be that I was one of the best actors that ever did it.

Jeffrey Wright is one of my favorite actors and I always wanted to work with him, so I was super excited that I was about to film alongside him. I still had two more weeks on *Armored* before *Cadillac* would start, so what did I do? I did the Beyoncé lemonade diet. I had to do action and all this shit, but I didn't eat for 14 days.

By day four, I didn't even care about food anymore. I had not one iota of a bite of food. I literally didn't consume anything but maple syrup, cayenne pepper and water. For 14 days, that's what I was surviving on, all in the spirit of getting wired to be Little Walter. You transform your body, you transform the performance. That's how I move.

By the time I got out to New York for my day one of *Cadillac Records*, they were already shooting. It was the scene that Beyoncé is all drugged out with Adrien Brody and they were breaking down in front of the fireplace. As soon as I landed in Newark Airport, there was a car waiting for me that drove me straight to set. I walked in and Beyoncé was doing that scene, so I sat there and watched from video village. As soon as they were done filming, I introduced myself to Adrien and Bey (even though I already knew her.)

"Hey, I know you know that I'm Columbus – but this is the last day you're going to see me," I said to Bey with a serious face. "I just want to give you a hug. For the rest of this shoot, I'm going to be Little Walter. Adrien, what's up boy? I'll see you later!"

They were laughing, thinking that I was playing, but I was so serious! I got back to my trailer and I knew the next day I was going to get to work and that these folks didn't know what was going to hit them! They were sleeping on me, and it put a chip on my shoulder and made me a better actor because I had something to fucking prove.

I shot all my older stuff first, so I had to go through two hours of hair and makeup and get the latex and it was just a grueling process. From the time I looked at myself and saw Little Walter, I talked like him all day — whether I was on camera or not. That entire 42-day shoot, I was him. He was me.

Playing Little Walter

Little Walter was a drinker and I am a method actor, so I became a drinker. Walter drank a pint of Jameson every day...so I drank a pint of Jameson every day. All day on set, I was sipping on something. I know it sounds crazy, but I evoked Little Walter's spirit in my body.

At first, people started taking notice and they were like, "This dude is either a genius or he's crazy." After a few days, I noticed that no one was really talking to me and I was getting some weird energy.

One day I went to rehearsal and it was me, Beyoncé, Adrien and Jeff. Of course I have a bottle in my hand, and Bey was laughing at me. I could tell she was thinking, "This nigga's really drinking right now!"

I was drinking all through that rehearsal. I went back to my trailer when we wrapped, and not too long after that, I heard a knock on my door. It was the director, Darnell.

"Hey, Columbus. Do you have a minute to talk?"

"Yeah, come on in baby!" I said in Walter's Southern drawl.

"Yeah, that's what I want to talk about!"

I could tell that she was about to hit me with some shit, but Little Walter wasn't really tripping.

"You're smoking and you're drinking, and this is unprofessional!"

"This is how I get down, baby!" I gave her all of that. "This is how I do my thing, baby!"

Unfortunately, all of that was all too much. She wanted none of that. Darnell just wasn't trying to hear it, and after a few minutes of back and forth, it made me break. I was pissed!

"Darnell, this is my process! You just pulled me out!" I said in my regular voice. "Either you're going to get with this process or I'm going home, because I'm going in on this one."

I honestly didn't expect the answer that I got.

"Well you can go home!"

She tried to fire me the first week. And she rounded up the other producers to help her do so thinking that they'd rally behind her but thankfully, they really fucked with me. They approached me later that day and asked me if I wanted to go home, but they also let me know that they really didn't want me to.

"Can you work with Darnell?"

"The question is can Darnell work with me?" I responded. "I don't have any issue with her! I am in character, I'm killing my role and I'm not bothering anybody."

They knew I was right.

"Just do your thing, stay locked in and keep doing your thing."

And with that they left me alone, but it still wasn't done. My agents were calling my phone not too long after.

"Columbus, we got a call from the producers and the director wants you off the set," I heard when I said hello. I didn't even get a greeting back. "What's going on over there?"

"Nothing is going on!" I shot back. "I'm in character and I'm doing what I need to do to play Little Walter. I already spoke to the producers and nobody is tripping. I'm just trying to do my job!"

"Yeah, we get it. Just do your thing and get out of there, then."

Cool, finally everyone was off my back. I couldn't believe that it was clear as day as to why I was smoking and drinking, and yet I was still getting shit for it! Did they give Heath Ledger shit when he was being crazy as The Joker? No! Method acting is not a new concept.

The next day, I was just hot. I came in to work with a real chip on my shoulder. I had the scene where I got my head smashed on the car by the police officers, and I studied that whole night. I couldn't even sleep I was so excited! It felt like I was playing in the Super Bowl; I knew I was going to go in and I was playing for keeps. I killed that fucking scene, but the next day I got a call from my agents and it looked like the drama was still coming.

"What the fuck are you doing out there?" was all I heard when I answered the phone.

"Dude, I'm doing my JOB! I'm working!" I was so exasperated at this point. "I'm trying to really build a character and really make this special!"

Their answer was the last thing that I expected.

"Jeffrey Wright's agent just called us," they said. Jeff and I were both at the talent agency CAA at the time. "He just said that Columbus Short just put down one of the best scenes he's ever been a part of in his entire career. Whatever you're doing, keep doing it. Jeffrey is obsessed with you!"

That was one of the dopest things I'd ever been told! Jeffrey was one of my favorite actors, and to get a compliment like that from him really meant the world. After that, me and Jeff were like best buds on set. Me, Jeff, and Adrien became quite close. It was a very memorable moment for me in my career. It can be so hard for black actors in Hollywood, and it honestly makes some of the older ones kind of like "fuck everybody" once they're on because it took so much to get there – including never having respect from their peers. So to have earned that respect at such a young age from two seasoned actors, it really went a long way for my confidence levels.

That was the great part of doing *Cadillac Records*. The downside is the part that never left.

Because I was in character for those 42 days, I was doing everything that Little Walter did except for the drugs. Like I mentioned, I was drinking a bottle of Jameson every day and smoking blunts every day. The last day of production was the day that I shot the dude for stealing my name. We were in Louisiana and I had to shoot the scene a few times. Not only was it the last day but this was my last scene too, and I remember specifically looking up and saying, "I'm going to miss you man," because I knew that I had to let Walter go. What I didn't know at the time was that it wasn't going to be that simple.

When we open up our spirit, actors and singers, we become basically a vessel to the craft and the creative spirit. I allowed my vessel for Little Walter's spirit to take over for that period of time, but what I realized later in my career was that you have to be very careful what spirits you allow in and how you release. I should have gone through a whole process before letting Little Walter go instead of just stopping cold turkey that one day. I'd been shooting for 42 days. It takes 21 days to create a habit – I did that twice over. I became an alcoholic just like him.

When I went back to L.A. when we were wrapped, I wasn't Little Walter anymore but I started to realize that a lot of him was still living in me. I still had that hot temper that he had. I still was smoking and drinking like crazy. I never stopped drinking after that except for the 30 days I did in rehab when I was on *Scandal* years later.

I shot *The Losers* a year later in the summer of 2009, but then I didn't work for a while after that until nearly a year later with *Scandal*. It was just crazy when I was out there in Puerto Rico and I kind of got this "partier" reputation, and no one really wanted to take a gamble on booking me. Even though I was partying with everyone else, everyone else was handling it like the professionals that they were. I wasn't waking up on time for work, I was showing up late. It was completely not me. I was dropping the ball and I think that kind of spread around Hollywood after *The Losers* like, "Columbus turns up and he'll be late." Nobody wants to book that guy. I truly am ashamed of that, I am better than that, wasn't raised or trained to behave like that.

I wholeheartedly believe I was still trying to repress the brokenness in myself and the void in my broken relationship, and I was looking to the bottle to do that. I think that with drugs and alcohol and all this stuff, you miss moments and you look back and think, "Damn! I missed so much!" I wish I would have slowed down and really enjoyed it and respected it and honored the blessing. It's a blessing to do what you love and get paid a lot of money for it. I think I took it for granted because it happened so fast.

I realized Little Walter hadn't left when I was in rehab in 2012, which was three years later. There are all these different types of therapies that you can take and I was doing this particular one called Eye Movement Deprivation Reprocessing. They use these lights and it's really popular with veterans to help them with their PTSD. It kind of takes you on a journey, and on the way, I saw Little Walter.

"Why are you still here?" I immediately questioned him.

The therapist told me to speak to my younger self.

"Tell him that you got this, that you can protect him," he added.

But I felt like it was really Little Walter that needed to be spoken to.

"Dude, what are you doing here? I can't carry you no more! It's over and I don't want this anymore!"

It was such a powerful revelation for me. After that, I went back to Season 3 of *Scandal* in a much better space! I had gotten the demon off my back and that's great, but that was really only one half of the battle. The issue was that even despite letting that go, I didn't change my environment.

The thing about rehab and recovery and when people change their lives is it's an ongoing process. You have to continue to do the work forever, and if you fall off, you're right back to where you started. So those old coping mechanisms came back and when I was stressed, I would just go to the bottle. But it started with a glass of wine or a shot every time I would argue with my girl or whatever and it went on from there again. I thought if I wasn't drinking Jameson, then it's cool; I'm not Little Walter. But then my anxiety got worse and I was drinking to cure my anxiety and it became this ugly vicious cycle that truthfully took me years to get over and break the curse.

Coming off the divorce with *that girl*, I was still kind of dabbling and doing things just to escape the drama. I was tired of the fighting, tired of being depressed, tired of the self-doubt and feelings of failure that crept into my mind on a continual basis. All of those things were just compiling in my spirit and it led me to want to escape whatever emotional reality I was having to deal with. I didn't want to do coke anymore, so alcohol seemed to be the remedy to chill me out.

The scariest part was that I was a very highly functional drinker. I could drink all day and function and get things done, but it came to a point where it was like okay, is this serving my life? What is it doing for my life? It wasn't helping my anxiety; it was exacerbating it. Alcohol wasn't my friend, and as time went on and this fact was made clear, it really made me really reflect within. What kind of life did I want?

Doing all of the analysis in my head, I started developing questions like, "What can come with me to this next chapter in my life? What has to be left in the past?" *That girl* needed to be left, my relationship with my mom and the strained relationship with my brothers needed to be left, my feelings being hurt whether right or not by those that I really cared about needed to be left, the first part of my career as a movie star – I needed to leave that too. Oh, and alcohol.

Alcohol was truthfully always a negative thing in my life. The first thing I did when all that stuff went down on *Scandal* was buy a bottle of chardonnay. Then I was drinking every day, all night long and doing coke and going through those dark days. Then that became my normal and that wasn't helping my life; it was time to move on. All of that stuff doesn't serve me now. All of my experiences have kind of culminated and lent themselves to the person I am today.

I'm proud to say that I'm sober and I've been sober for over A YEAR now. It hasn't been a struggle, either. It has been freeing. I prayed. I literally was so tired of drinking that it became this thing where I'm like, why do I have to wake up and drink so I can function? Why do I have to do this? Laying down that last little thing of my past was paramount for me to break into this new book that is shaping up to be my life. It's exciting and it's a blessing. I'm happy and while I do know that happiness can be fleeting, I would say I'm content and at peace with my wife and our life. It's amazing what God has done.

My son, Denz

Evander Holyfield told me his mother used to always tell him, "If you don't pick up nothing, you won't ever have to put it down." Unfortunately, in my journey I picked up some habits that were not useful and were only detrimental to everything I wanted to do with my life.

To wake up every morning and be excited about the day and what I can do to progress or for my family as a husband and father or a career man, a creative – it's caused my creativity, my patience and my clarity to truly blossom. There are so many positives and I'm not here to simply say that drinking is bad for everybody, but it's just something that I thought was not an issue, yet it was slowing me down. It was causing me to get into this depressing funk and carrying that on your back as part of a generational curse in my family? Well, I wanted to be the one to break it.

I'm grateful today to say that I have and I want to continue to pass that on to my children.

15

THE ART OF F14

Jail is not somewhere that I've ever aspired to be. I think that I can confidently assume that's also the general consensus. And while I'll be the first to admit that I've made some poor decisions in my life, I can say that I've managed to keep myself out of the system for the most part. Unfortunately, we can't always control external forces, and *that girl* is the main reason why I did my first time in county.

As I spoke about earlier, I had missed a surprise court date that my ex-wife sprung on me while I was in Barbados for a charity event. I tried working with my lawyer on it because I couldn't miss this prior engagement, but that didn't work out. When I got back to L.A., I had a warrant and I had to go to court. I can admit, though, that I wasn't respecting the court the way that I should have. So please take it from me: you've got to respect the courts. Whether you're guilty or not guilty, show up to your court dates! It's only going to hurt you in the end, and you're not going to prove anything to anyone. You might be able to dodge the inevitable for a little while, but that it is going to catch up with you. Take it from me.

The judges were trying to make an example out of me and teach me a lesson because like I said, I wasn't respecting the court and I wasn't showing up to my dates. Being that I'd missed the date while I was away and then another one after that, I was basically forced to take a plea deal that included a choice between 45 days in jail or 30 days of community labor. It should probably go without saying that I opted for the latter. There were also some other super fun stipulations sprinkled in that included a year's worth of weekly domestic violence classes, 22 Alcoholics Anonymous meetings, being banned from owning a gun for a decade and the best one of all: three years of probation.

I wasn't guilty and I will stand by that forever, but I didn't have the time nor the money to go to trial to prove *that girl* was lying – you know, because she'd drained it all from my account which got us to where we were then in the first place. Unfortunately, when you don't have the money to fight and you need to keep your job, you end up taking a deal. It's a fucked up situation all around. It's even more fucked up when you're a public figure.

"Columbus Short pleads no contest to domestic violence, avoids jail," was the headline in the *LA Times*. My kids can see these things on the internet forever, and that's just something that I have to live with. And I can put the blame on a lot of things, but at the end of the day I played a role in that as well. It is what it is.

Now I know that I started this story referring to *that girl* being the reason I did my first time in county, and none of the above referenced any jail time. That's because there's so much more in this never-ending saga.

So, about a week before the fight in my house with *that girl* that led to the above court drama, I was involved in another situation that led to more court drama that eventually tied in with the other court drama. Yeah, I know. My life is a movie that nobody wanted to see!

My brother's ex-fiancée was best friends with *that girl* and my brother and his ex had my nephew, Marley. He's a cool little dude; we call him Mars. They broke up but *that girl* and her were still best friends and being that she's my nephew's mother, she's still family in a way. She was engaged to this new guy at this time and was having an engagement party. *That girl* and I were already on the outs, but she asked me if I'd go with her to the party and I agreed. Why I went is a question I still don't really have a clear-cut answer for, even years later.

I guess it was because I really loved her. Well, what I understood of love. I have no other explanation as to why I would go back to her time and time again and then go to things with her, especially like this. I think maybe it was selfish on my part, but I really did love her. I really did care about her soul and her well-being and all those things. I'm not in love with her now, but I still care about this person. You know, you spend 12 years with someone and create a child with them – even if they're evil, I love the good in her and that's just how I'm built. That's why I was there.

I went to the party and keep in mind — I hadn't seen my brother's ex or her family in a very long time because I'd been on *Scandal*. That being said, a lot of things in my life had changed since I'd last seen them. I played a lot of golf with her dad and her older brother, Tone, in the past. We were a very close family, but Tone thought (and probably still thinks) that he's some kind of gang member and he was antagonizing me while I was there like, "Oh Mr. Big Shot! Oh, you too good for us?"

I don't take well to antagonizing. I was telling him that he needed to chill, and eventually, he told me that he wanted to buy me a drink.

"I'm cool, bro. I'm not drinking right now," I told him.

I had just finished rehab the season before so I was on the straight and narrow.

In Tone's pursuit to get me to drink, he ends up knocking a glass of wine onto *that girl*, but she doesn't go off like she normally does. I thought that was rather odd, and then she proceeds to tell me not to trip or react.

"Yo Tone, do we have to have a conversation, bro?" My patience was wearing thinner by the moment.

"Oh, you Mr. Big Shot!" he said again as he put me in a headlock and walked me outside into the back alley. I think everybody in the party thought he was joking because, as I said, we'd had this long-standing relationship like brothers. So, he was wasted and he walked me out there, and in my head, I already knew that I was knocking him out as soon as we got outside. I'd had it at that point.

As soon as we got through the door and he let me go, I just took off on him. I knocked him out cold and as he was on the ground, everybody started rushing outside. He was unconscious — like damn near dead — and I started freaking out like, "Did I kill Tone?!" It was serious.

His dad came out, and I started apologizing profusely when he responded, "Get in your car and get out of here! We'll deal with this; it's a family matter. The police are on their way. Get out of here."

So, I went home. I had his father's blessing, so I wasn't about to wait around to find out what could happen next.

The next day, my lawyer called me and told me that the police were looking for me.

"Listen, you're going to have to turn yourself in."

Yeah, not the words that I wanted to hear. I was still working on *Scandal* at the time and I had to be on set the next day, so I went to Monrovia to turn myself in with the thought process that I'd be in and out and back to work. No problem there; the plan works, but when I got to set, I immediately got called into the office. There's yet another headline, and I'd been previously told by Shonda that they didn't want any more fucking headlines.

Actor Columbus Short In Need Of Real Life Olivia Pope After Bar Fight, was one of the more creative headlines I read. This one was from The Urban Daily:

"Actor Columbus Short might be taking his role as one of Olivia Pope's gladiators a little too seriously. The actor who plays Harrison Wright on the hit ABC drama 'Scandal' is now being investigated by police after getting into a bar fight."

As the story goes, Short was at an L.A. establishment called Gabe's Bar & Grill. He was celebrating the engagement of his friends. Things were going smoothly until Short got into an argument with a guy at the bar. The other bar patron was heard screaming rude things to Short like, 'You might be richer than me but I get my girls to buy me everything I want including your wife.' When the actor heard that, he came from behind the guy and punched him in the face.

Columbus Short must pack a pretty mean punch because

the guy was said to have gotten his nose broken from the punch and he was knocked unconscious for a few minutes as well. After Short clocked the dude, he left the bar immediately. Columbus Short's 37-year-old opponent was taken to a nearby hospital and now cops are investigating Short for criminal battery."

This one just one of the many headlines that were hurting my case for another season! Needless to say, *Scandal* didn't renew my contract the following month. 2014 was epic.

If you're keeping score, now I have that case at the same time that I'm on probation for *that girl*. Two weeks later when I kicked her out of the house, she went and teamed up with Tone and they decided to merge their cases. Now I had a case at LAX and one in Van Nuys.

It took quite some time to actually get the court dates, and now we're fast forwarding to about a year-and-a-half to two years later. I'd finished all of my community service and my meetings and all of that good stuff, but at this time, I was absolutely still on probation. I was also not on *Scandal* anymore and I was living in Atlanta, so I was flying back and forth to L.A. for these court dates.

On a particular day, I had court in LAX and in Van Nuys on the same day. I didn't know which to go to first, so I went to Van Nuys first but they didn't pull my case number up until about an hour before noon. I knew that as long as I got to LAX by 1:30 that I wouldn't have a warrant, but they broke for lunch in Van Nuys and came back and it's nearly 1:30. It's getting spooky.

I'm still fairly calm at the moment, because I still think that maybe just maybe I could get down to LAX before they close the court up at 2 p.m. and explain the situation. I finish my business in Van Nuys and the D.A. goes, "Mr. Short has a warrant out of LAX right now, so I think he should be remanded."

They put me in jail.

I was immediately hauled out in cuffs and taken to the bus to head to county. Now mind you, I had absolutely no idea – not even a small thought – that I'd be going to jail that day. I can't exactly theorize how one would dress in preparation for jail, but I can definitely tell you that my outfit that day would not fall into that category. I'd come into court on my preppy hipster swag, ankles out and all. I had khakis with the pants legs rolled up, an argyle sweater — the whole nine. No one ever wants to go to jail but at least some people know when to expect it. I literally had no idea. I got on the bus like, "Oh shit. I'm going to real, actual jail!"

I don't know what I expected to see when I got down to county, but it was more of a mess than I can even describe. It's just something else. You get strip searched and then you get thrown into what they call the fish tank. I was in the tank with hours passing by, and eventually I fell asleep on the concrete floor to pass the time. (*Really super comfortable*, said no one ever.) When I woke up, there were a group of Latino dudes just staring at me.

"We know who you are," one guy said in a very feminine voice. "Don't worry. Nobody's going to do nothing to you here. Put your sweater over your face – you don't want to let these motherfuckers see you sleep!"

It was at that moment that I realized I was in the gay tank. I don't know if they profiled me based on what they're used to seeing; I was dressed homosexually that day, I guess.

The way that the process works is that you sit in the tank until you get called up to the window to assign you to your cell. I finally got called up, and I walked up to get my wristband and my inmate number and all that, and as I was walking up, some deputies were walking four black dudes back to their cells. These dudes looked young, probably between the ages of 19 and 21, and they started going wild as soon as they saw me.

"Oh snaps!" one dude yelled out in a thick Los Angeles accent. "Oh, that's that nigga right there!"

The deputies started looking at me, and I was looking at them looking at me looking at them.

"Who are you?" they demanded.

"I don't know. I'm just here."

They didn't respond to me, but instead continued to walk the guys down to where they were headed. I got my wristband and headed back into the gay tank, but it wasn't long before those same deputies came back over to look for me.

"Come here," one of them said. "What's your name?"

"Columbus," I responded.

"Who are you?"

I repeated my name again, but that wasn't what they were looking for.

"No, who are you? How do those guys know you?"

"I have no idea."

"Mm-hmm. No idea, huh?"

Five minutes later, they grabbed me and told me that they were moving me. They walked me down and I could see through the door that it was all Crips in the tank that I was being led to. It was the Crip tank.

You know those western movies when you walk into the saloon or something and you're the black guy in the South and the jukebox abruptly stops upon your entry? That's exactly what it was like when they opened the gate. All the Locs were in there loud and hyped up, and as soon as I came in, it was radio silence and everybody was staring at me. It was like I got thrown into the shark tank!

I grew up around gang bangers so I wasn't shook, but at the same time, I didn't want any smoke! They started asking where I was from and I let them know that I was from around the way, so of course then they started asking if I knew people from around there, naming their cousins Lil Scoot Scoot and them. Then out of nowhere, an OG from the back spoke up.

"Aye, hold up cuh! I know this nigga right here, cuh!" he said. "That's that nigga from *Stomp the Yard*, cuh!"

Everybody in the whole tank went crazy! "Oh, that *is* that nigga!"

It completely turned into a full reunion! These niggas start asking me a billion questions – and I wasn't about to gamble with not answering. Let's get this press conference started, guys.

"How was it kissing Meagan Good?"

"Do a stomp for us real quick!"

"Oh you was in that other movie *This Christmas* huh, cuh?!"

The sheriffs walked by 20 minutes later and they saw me holding court! I was telling stories like I was a kindergarten teacher talking to my little class in a circle around my feet, and we were really in there kicking it! At one point, though, a couple of OGs ended up sitting me down.

"All of us in here, we ain't finna see no light of day," one of them began. "We don't want to see you up in here, bro. This is not where you're supposed to be. We got you while you're in here, but do your time, get out of here and do the right thing."

It really impacted me hearing that from dudes that didn't have shit to lose. Those guys were about to go away for life and never see the light of day again, so it was really impactful. Serendipitously enough, the sheriffs came and got me shortly after that conversation and they finally gave me my jumpsuit. If you're in regular GP (general population), you wear a blue jumpsuit. But if you're high-powered like a Suge Knight or some kind of high-profile celebrity case, then they'll give you an orange jumpsuit and put you in HP (high power). They ended up giving me an orange jumpsuit but didn't really say anything to me as they did, so I got the feeling that I was about to be in a pretty interesting area.

I got to the row and it was literally like a scene out of a movie. (Clearly a reoccurring theme in my life.) I was in F row and walking past cells and the first one I see has Too $hort in it! He was in there for 30 days for some DUI or random shit. Then I saw the old man that killed mad people – he's a serial killer. I think they called him the Night Stalker or something. Then the actor that killed his wife that was on that cop show, he was in there too.

They were walking me down past 10, 11, 12, 13 and then they opened up F14. I went in there and there was this beautiful mural on the walls of the cell. It was crazy!

"This art is amazing!" I said when I walked in. "Whoever was in here was amazing!"

"Your boy was in here," the deputy responded.

"My boy?" I asked. I was pretty positive that I didn't have any homies that went to county any time recently, so

I was really curious as to what their answer was about to be.

"This was Chris Brown's cell!"

They gave me my boy Breezy's cell, and I'm not sure if they were trying to be funny because we'd been in films together, but I actually really appreciated it. I used the time to read a lot and I just started adding on to his unfinished mural. The deputies actually fucked with it so much that as I was leaving, they told me, "It's really dope. We're leaving it up."

Chris Brown and I

Unless they took it down – which I would doubt – there is a cell in county right now on F row designed by Chris Brown and Columbus Short. It's honestly a very small silver lining in an otherwise extremely fucked up story, but I'd like to think that it's giving whoever is occupying F14 now and in the future at least something to do if they're artistic. At the very least, it gives them something to look at and maybe even provide some source of inspiration or hope. Art is truly a universal language and in my darkest days, it was literally all I had. Though it's small, I hope that our art can be that source for someone else.

16

WHEN IVERSON CROSSED JORDAN

Denzel Washington is the only actor I ever really wanted to go head-to-head with on screen, and still do. You know, Sidney Poitier was Denzel's first image as a forefather and Denzel was mine. I admire him so much that I named my son after him — but it's not solely based on the fact that he is one of the most amazing actors of our time. It's also because of how he played me.

After *Stomp the Yard* was number one two weekends in a row, I basically had my pick of roles. I was the guy now. I had big league agents and I was making big league moves. My agency CAA called me one day and told me that I was going to meet with famed casting director Deb Aquila and Denzel Washington. They wanted me to test for *Great Debaters* on Universal.

As soon as they sent me the script, I started studying

it profusely. You cannot come to Denzel Washington and not be on your game because he will literally open up his mouth, devour you and spit you out. That dude is a monster, and I had to be ready to take him on...and I knew I could. Not only was I secure in my skillset, but I had an even bigger advantage because I was a real-life student of argumentary debate. I had literally competed on debate teams in school, and now a role built around that with the one person I'd always wanted to work with was at my feet. Almost immediately after they sent the script, I started asking when this meeting was going to happen.

"He's wrapping up *American Gangster* right now, and when he gets back in town in the next couple of weeks, you two and the execs at Universal are going to meet," CAA told me at first.

Two weeks went by. Nothing. Three weeks. Still nothing. Finally it had been a month since this conversation, and I was itching! At this point I had to call my agents to ask what was happening because there was no reason for it to be taking that long. Then I get the call back from them with an update.

"Denzel is on a Sabbatical."

Man, what?

Right after I get the news about this "sabbatical," I was randomly talking with a friend of mine who just so happens to be Lenny Kravitz's niece, and she was telling me about how she was with her uncle and "Denz." Mind you, she's somewhere on the Eastern Seaboard — nowhere near where I am.

"Denz who?" I asked, because somehow I just knew what her answer was going to be, despite how random it seemed.

"Denzel Washington."

"Nah, you've got to be kidding me," I responded incredulously. "I'm supposed to be meeting him!"

She proceeds to tell me how "Denz" and Lenny have this whole friendship thing happening and that they were hanging out while her uncle was on tour. In other words, I'm not going to see Denz for a while. I was so ready for him, and now I was forced to wait. All that did was put a bigger chip on my shoulder, though, so when we finally did meet, I came in there with something to prove. Now I got some work for you, *Denz*. You're playing with me, and I'm coming to slice your Achilles off, bruh! You have to pump yourself up that way when going in to battle, seek and destroy.

The next month, I finally got the call that the meeting was happening. I will never forget how I felt the night before — I know this script like the back of my hand and I'm about to blow Denzel Washington's socks off. I had already made this scenario in my head that when we'd meet, he'd see something in me. He was going to take me under his wing and he was going to guide me through this crazy labyrinth of Hollywood, passing the torch to this young diamond in the rough.

I walked into the room to test, and it was myself, Jurnee Smollett and all of the producers on the movie. I couldn't wait for this moment. This was literally the moment I'd been dreaming about my entire life. I was about to sit down and give Denzel Washington that work, and then he was going to see how great I was and take me under his wing.

Denzel came in late and told Jurnee to sit down. The tension was so thick in the room that you could cut it with a knife, and it was impossible to read him at this point. Thankfully, the execs broke the ice.

"Oh Columbus, congratulations! *Stomp the Yard* was number one two weekends in a row? Wow, that is amazing!" they gushed. "You were great in the movie!"

They were just showering me with adoration at that point, but it didn't last long.

"Okay!" Denzel commanded. "Okay! Enough! Enough of that."

It was just me and him now. All the producers, the actors, the directors – they were behind us and now it was just me versus him. He turned the New York baseball cap he was wearing to the back as he looked me in the eyes and grabbed the front of my folding chair to slide it right up to him. We were knee to knee, and I knew that he was trying to intimidate me, but I was unmovable. A lot of men would have been scared about that, but I wasn't. He laughed.

"Once a Roman general, Mr. Lowe?" he prompted me.

That was the start of the monologue that I was supposed to say. This man really thought that I wasn't going to rise to the occasion. Not me. Not Columbus Short.

"Once a Roman general," I said with a confidence that came from so deep. I stared Denzel in the face and vomited that monologue out on his knees.

"Stand up!" he commanded with his infamous laugh when I finished. "Once a Roman general, Mr. Lowe?"

I spit it again perfectly. He laughed.

"Go over there!" he told me, pointing to another part of the room. "Once a Roman general, Mr. Lowe?"

I do it again, not taking my eyes off of him. That's a predator in the room, and I'm on his neck. He laughed when I finished.

"Come on and sit down, boy," he said kindly, motioning toward my chair. He shook me there. I don't know what it was, but he shook me.

"Once a Roman general..." I started out, and I did it different this time. My cadence was lower, more direct.

By now, the tension was even more high in the room. I know the execs were thinking, "We're staying out of the way. This is black on black crime! This must be a black rite of passage or something."

"Haaaa! Okay, okay!" Denzel said when I finished, and he brought Jurnee back in for us to do the entire scene.

There was nothing I could have done better. It was me versus my hero and I was ready and he wasn't. And just as I figured, the producers told my agents at CAA that they had never in their lives seen someone battle Denzel like I did. Columbus Short had given Denzel Washington that work. The very next morning, I was told to standby for an offer later that day.

Nothing came, though.

I wasn't worried, but the next morning, I was confused. My texts were filled with congratulatory messages about landing this film and I hadn't told a soul. And I still had no offer. What is happening? As it turned out, *Variety* had run a headline that said Denzel Washington and Columbus Short will star in *The Great Debaters*.

"Principle photography is scheduled to commence mid-May, with Columbus Short (*Stomp the Yard*), in negotiations to play one of Tolson's students," the February 2007 article read.

I was confused because my agents hadn't told me anything about negotiations or having landed the role, but if *Variety* was saying it, I must have it! Right? I didn't know how Hollywood worked at the time, so I really just thought that I could get excited now. I wanted to take down the best; even Iverson had to cross Jordan at one point. I had to cross Denz, and that stands to date — since this would actually be the reason why I haven't gotten to yet.

Another day went by and while I was receiving even more congratulatory texts, I didn't have an offer. I had to call my agents to know what was going on, and finally they called me back with the film's producer Todd Black on three-way.

"Hey, I just want to say you did an amazing job last week," Todd said.

Here it comes. Here's my offer.

"I mean you brought it; just unbelievable work!"

Come on, Todd. Say it!

"Unfortunately, we're not going to be going further."

But the announcement. *Variety.* What is happening?! I started to bring it up, and he cut me off before I could even finish my sentence.

"That's the problem."

Apparently, Denzel had gone into the office fuming the morning after the article came out, slammed *Variety* on the desk and screamed, "Who hired this kid?! I didn't fucking hire this kid!"

"This is the guy we loved," they responded, "We ran the numbers!"

"If this is my picture, *I do the hiring*," Denz said. "I hire my actors. I didn't pick this kid! I want to see other actors.'

And just like that, it was over. To this day, I don't know

who put out the announcement. I feel like it was CAA trying to campaign, but they clearly made a wrong move because you can't fuck with Denzel.

I found out later that Nate Parker wrote him a four-page letter basically gently stroking all the best parts of Denzel's ego and booked the job. Denzel wanted to work with him because he knew that Nate wasn't the guy that was going to come for his throne. He was a safe, talented actor but he wasn't a threat to Denz. Nate was not taking Denzel's throne. It's been over a decade since then and as you can see, my statements aren't hate – just fact. In fairness, he's a wonderful director and turned in a strong performance in *Birth of a Nation*!

As you'd probably imagine, I was absolutely crushed at this point – but then I got *Armored*. Now I was working with Matt Dillon, Jean Reno and Laurence Fishburne and I was the lead! And there was a young actor and director on set by the name of Malcolm Mays. He was 19 at the time and following me around the Sony lot nearly every day because Sony had given him an offer to groom him to be a future film maker as a part of some program. He's on a show called *Snowfall* now. He's amazing.

I was on a lunch break one day on *Armored*, and Malcolm made his way into my trailer.

"Columbus, you're not going to believe who's here doing ADR!"

ADR is Audio Visual Recording. "Who?" I asked.

"Denzel! He's doing ADR in the Judy Garland building!"

"Man, fuck Denz. He knows I'm coming for him." I was really over him at that point because everything was still fairly fresh to me.

He laughs and he leaves, but thirty minutes later – Malcolm's back.

"I told Denzel that you're down here and you guys should say what's up!" Malcolm told me. I didn't know if this was just Denz or if Malcolm had run his mouth about my previous sentiments, but his response was pretty interesting.

"I don't gotta see that little nigga," Malcolm told me Denzel said. "I've seen a lot of niggas come and go. Let's see if that little nigga stays."

"Denzel said those exact words?" I asked, stunned. "Malcolm, say exactly what Denzel said."

He repeated it back, word for word.

"He said, 'I don't gotta see that little nigga. I've seen a lot of niggas come and go. Let's see if that little nigga stays.'"

Instantly, I got hot all over again! Why was this nigga tripping on me? ME?

I didn't see him that day, nor the next, nor any time at all while I was on the *Armored* set. I just eventually pushed that incident to the back of my mind and wasn't thinking about running into him at all anymore. About six months to a year went by, and my career was moving at the trajectory that it was supposed to be moving at. I was doing all of these movies, but I got a call from my agents one day with an interesting proposition.

"You know Columbus, we know you said you want to go back on stage..." they started.

My dream was and still is to get an EGOT. I need that. I want an Emmy, a Grammy, an Oscar and a Tony Award. I can do it all, and I know I can earn that.

"You can start working on your EGOT if you go do *Fences* with Denzel," they continued.

They wanted me to fly to New York to meet with him to discuss doing the 2010 Broadway revival of the play, but I was way too skeptical at that point. I was going to fly myself out there to be given the runaround? Nah, they had the wrong one.

I sat on it and I prayed on it for a couple of days, and I started to come around. Maybe I caught Denz on a bad day, you know? I should give this a shot because whatever it is, I can work through it. If I can work with Denz on stage, then maybe my dream, my vision of him being paramount in my career and my life would come into realization.

"Before I go out to New York, I want to get on a phone call with Denzel," I said when I called my agents back. "I want to hear where he's at!"

My agents assured me that it wouldn't be an issue,

and that they'd reach out to Denzel's agent, Ed Limato. Turns out, it was an issue. Surprise, surprise.

"There's no way I'm going to get Denzel on a call with Columbus," Ed told them. "It's just not going to happen. Denzel is not going to do that."

At this point, the hell with it! I was already of the mindset that I wanted to speak with him, so now I wasn't just going to give up and walk away. I've never done that in my life, so I wasn't about to start with Denzel Washington. I decided I was going to get on my Nate Parker flow and write Denz a four-page letter of my own, but my letter wasn't going to be as flattering.

Mr. Washington,

I remember the day like it was yesterday when I got the call that we were going to be meeting on 'Great Debaters.' I remember the feeling that I had the night before actually coming to meet you. I remember feeling like an NFL player on Super Bowl Sunday about to come out of the tunnel ready to play for a championship! I was looking forward to you being that mentor, that OBiKNOBE to my Luke Skywalker, but you disappointed me. Not only did you break my heart, but I gave you my all! I left my blood in that room and you toiled with me.

I got your message from Malcolm about how you've seen a lot of little niggas come and go and you want to see if this little nigga is going to stay. I promise you, Denzel, that whether you help me out or not, whether you respect me or not, I'm going to stay. I'm here to stay. So, if you would like to speak before I get my own plane ticket to come out there and meet you in New York, I would like to speak to you.

Best,

Columbus Short

Of course there are some things omitted for time restraints, but you get the point!

I sent it off just before Thanksgiving. The entertainment business as a whole pretty much shuts down from December 15 until a few weeks into the new year for the holidays, so I honestly wasn't anticipating a response for some time. Yet and still on Christmas Eve morning, my phone went off at 7 a.m. from a restricted phone number.

I never picked up restricted calls, and I certainly wasn't starting on Christmas Eve. But I was still with *that girl* at the time, and she wasn't into that idea at all.

"What bitch is calling you restricted this early in the morning?" she screamed at me. Ah, what a lovely way to start our holiday. "Pick it up!"

She didn't win that one, but moments later when I got the notification that I have a voicemail, she insisted that I check it on speaker phone! I knew that I was rolling the dice, but I was not about to argue on Christmas Eve. Here goes nothing.

I pressed play, and "I'm trying to reach Columbus..." is coming through my phone speaker. Denzel Washington was speaking on my voicemail. "I got your letter."

He gave me a 323 number to call him at, and then I hear the click. This man had to have been on a rotary phone because I could hear him physically hanging up the phone. It was an aggressive hang-up.

"Oh shit!" I yelled to *that girl*, "Denzel just called me!"

Her demeanor had changed from a screwed-up battle rapper face to a little kid's face on Christmas morning, and even though I was extremely pre-occupied with the important matter at hand, a little part of me still found time to gloat that she was proven really, really wrong.

She told me to hurry up and call him back and obviously, that was the plan. I re-played the message to get the number again since I'd been way too distracted to take it down the first time and put it in my phone to press send.

"I'm trying to reach Mr. Washington," I said to the elderly Hispanic woman who answered the phone.

"Okay, hold on please."

I was put on hold for about five minutes, and it was a long five minutes. Let me note that I literally called back thirty seconds after he left that voicemail.

"Mr. Washington is not available," she said when she finally came back to the phone. "He will call you back. What's your number?"

This guy. I told her that he had my number and hung up, and then I just left it alone. I didn't want to be thirsty, but by New Year's Day when I hadn't heard back, I decided to call the number again. The same thing happened and again, I didn't hear anything. Why would he call me and then not call me back? Denzel really be playing some games, so at this point, it was screw Denzel Washington once again!

Less than a year later, I found myself on set of my film *The Losers*, asking Idris Elba, "How was it working with Denz? I feel like he's a dick!" Admittedly I was kind of obsessed with hearing others validate the same thoughts that I had developed on Denzel. I guess it made me feel less angry to hear that it wasn't just me that he was an asshole to; he was an equal opportunity asshole.

"He's a fucking dick, bro!" he said in his British accent, which somehow made it more validating. "He's a fucking dick!"

Naturally I had to ask what happened, and he proceeded to tell me about an incident on set of *American Gangster* in 2006. During the scene where Idris and Denzel are at the diner and he offered to pay the bill or whatever it is, Denz had actually tried to check him in real life. Denzel is a bully! He likes to bully people on set and in that particular moment he told Idris, "Don't do that again on the next take."

According to Idris, he responded, "You're not going to tell me about my acting choices, bruv. You're not going to make acting choices for me. I'ma do my thing, you do your thing and we see what happens."

Idris is a Virgo like me, so he wasn't and still isn't

scared of Denzel. And after they did the take and Idris did the opposite of what Denzel told him to do, it was game-on.

The next scene they filmed was when Denzel pulls the gun on Idris and shoots him in the forehead, he tells me. In any production, you do a fifteen-minute safety meeting whenever there's a gun on set, especially if you're doing a point-blank shoot. You have to put the gun over to the right so that the shell pops off and you have like a four-foot distance from the head because it's a muzzle flash. It didn't happen like that, though.

"Bruv, he pushes the gun into my forehead and pulls the trigger point blank!" Idris said, seemingly still shocked at what happened. "I went black! Columbus, I thought the fucking guy shot me in the head for real. It felt like I got shot in the head. I thought I was dead! That shit shocked me out! They shut production down because everybody thought I was shot. I'm literally bleeding from my forehead."

When he came to, he told me that he saw Denzel getting in his Maybach, driving back to base camp like nothing had happened. About an hour later, Idris was at craft services getting some food when Denzel came up behind him.

"I would have never let nobody do that to me," Denzel said in his ear.

"You did that to me!" Idris responded. "Bruv if we weren't on a movie set, I'd fuck you up right now!"

They actually had to break them up, but no real physical damage was done. I remember thinking if that was me, the old me...I would have broken his jaw, no questions asked, which would have abruptly ended my career.

Three years later in 2012, I'm on the number one television show on network television, *Scandal.*

Tisha Campbell and Duane Martin have a club in Studio City, and Thursdays was industry night. You could catch anybody there – Will and Jada, obviously Tisha and Duane; it was a who's who of names. This particular Thursday night, I got off work on *Scandal* early, so I ended up stopping by the spot on my way home with my boy.

I saw Denzel right away.

"There's your man!" my boy tells me as soon as we walked in. And there he was, sitting at a table smoking a cigar, surrounded by like ten real Russian mob dudes. This dude is really cold with it in real life!

"There *is* my mans right there," I replied, not taking my eyes off Denz. "Let me go say something."

At that point, I didn't care I was going up to him. And when I did, I was greeted with a handshake and a subtle smile.

"You never called me back!" I demanded.

"Oh no, yeah!" You know, it's that whole spiel.

"It's all good. I appreciate that you actually read my letter."

He asked me what I was working on currently and in my head, I was like, "Man, you know what I'm working on! You talk to Kerry! You know what it is! Don't play with me!" But of course, I'ma play the game.

"I'm working on *Scandal* with Kerry," I said with a big fake smile.

"Oh yeah, that's right!" he replied. "Okay, alright! Well keep up the good work!" That was the last time I saw Denz. I doubt he'll ever know how much those small few words of encouragement meant to me.

I always felt like Denzel was trying to "little nigga" me and it bothered me my whole career. So much so that years later that very notion became the reason behind my son's name. When my now-wife was pregnant with our son, he was kicking a lot in her stomach. When I went to look up names that have a "wild one" type of meaning to them, ironically enough, one of the names that came up was Denzel! I told my wife right then and there that that's what his name would be. She asked me why.

"Because now Denzel is my little nigga."

The truth is he remains to be my favorite actor, period. He is brilliant in all his choices on screen, and after years seeking his validation of my existence in the business, I am finally at peace with it all and still would jump at the chance to share the screen with him. My son carries my hero's name; he's destined for greatness!

17

A DEVIL'S PLAYGROUND

True to the Game Press on Wendy Williams' Show

2 014 was a wild time. All of the drama with *that girl* had worn me so thin that I couldn't even focus on anything. It had all caught up to me. *Scandal* got one too many headlines from your boy and opted not to renew my contract that April. Season 3 was my last and I went out with a bang – kind of literally. Harrison was held at

gunpoint by hating ass Rowan and the Secret Service as the show ended.

The season finale did numbers with 10.5 million viewers. It was cool to go out on a high note like that, but having to leave the show isn't exactly the highest note. It just wasn't working on either end with all of the drama that I just couldn't seem to avoid, and so I had to step.

"At this time I must confirm my exit from a show I've called home for 3 years, with what is the most talented ensemble on television today," my exiting statement read. "I would like to first thank Shonda Rhimes for the opportunity to work with such an amazing cast. Thank you GLADIATORS, who have supported me throughout my entire career and of course to ABC and Shondaland for allowing me to play such a pivotal role in the *Scandal* series. I have enjoyed every single minute of it. Everything must come to an end, and unfortunately the time has come for Harrison Wright to exit the canvas. I wish nothing but the best for Shonda, Kerry and the rest of the cast, who have become like a second family to me in such a short amount of time. For this, I will forever be grateful."

Swag

I really, truly was grateful for the family that I'd built there. I don't know where I would be today if they weren't there to save me that day on set when shit went all the way left.

I moved to Arizona for a period of time after wrapping to try to get my mind right. AZ did what it was supposed to do; I got my strength back, I detoxed. I feel like throughout my life, Arizona has consistently been the place I duck off to in order to get right and clear my head. It's something about the desert. I felt good – good enough to try to come back to Los Angeles.

That didn't last very long.

It was just some weird energy when I got back to my city, so I felt like I needed a way bigger change than Arizona. I wasn't sure what to do exactly, though, so I started this period of being a bit of a nomad. I had no job and nothing better to do, so why not?

I started hanging wherever the wind would take me for a few months. I'd do a few weeks here, a few weeks there, but then I got into this altercation in Dallas and that kind of put a quick end to that stay. As you can probably assume, I racked up another headline. If there was one thing that I was good at, keeping my name in the media was one of them, huh? If only it was for something a little more positive.

It was the 4th of July in Dallas and one thing led to another while I was at a bar. The detox I'd gone through in Arizona didn't really last too long and to quote the police report, I "got into an issue" with security. I was ultimately arrested for public intoxication, and of course every write-up about it made sure to mention the rest of the shit I'd already been in thus far that year.

My homie Big Block of Block Entertainment in Atlanta caught the TMZ headline about the incident and called me the next day. (I was appropriately dressed for the holiday and they ran with, "*Columbus Short Shows True Stripes During Bar Arrest.*" Touché.)

"Bro, what is going on?" Block said when I picked up the phone. "Come out here and work on music and get your head right, man. You need to get away from all this bullshit."

Block had a beautiful house in Buford and I knew

that made the most sense for me. So, I picked up and headed over to ATL. Funny enough, the plan was to get my mind right but instead I lost my mind out there. It was like an episode of the Atlanta Thots. I dove into that scene head-first out there, and let me tell you – there was a LOT to dive into. That shit was a movie.

I had gotten to this frame of mind like, fuck it. At this point, I was already public enemy number one for head-line after headline – so why not really wild out and live up to the hype? I might as well be a bad boy if you think I'm a bad boy. I hate to say it now, but it was almost in that sense like, I didn't give a fuck. I just wanted to do my music and live my life. I was tired of the judgement, tired of the headlines, tired of the stress and the pressure of everything.

That was an interesting time. I grew exponentially as an artist, as a writer, as a musician. Maybe the best part was that I got to see what these thots are really like now, though. It's a whole new world out here. And I'm not saying that as if I was happy to just be out here thotting around, I'm saying that to say that it really opened my eyes to what I have NOT been missing. These crazy chicks! They're not all crazy but these girls with that spirit, that energy — that's a different kind of species. Which leads me to this next particular chapter in my life.

After running through everything (and by that, I mean everyone) in Atlanta, I made my way back to Los

Angeles because I knew that was where I really needed to be to work and figure shit out. I continued to work on music, and I got with Ne-Yo and his Compound camp to write for them. Ne-Yo and I had been cool for years since *SLD2* and *Stomp the Yard*, and he welcomed me with open arms when I came back around. He's always been a real one. While I was getting back into the swing of things, I ended up getting approached to do this movie, *True to The Game*. It was an adaptation of the popular Teri Woods novel, with Preston A. Whitmore II on board to direct and Vivica A. Fox signed on to star.

Ne-Yo and I

Keyshia Cole's former manager Manny Halley (who

you may remember from her reality show, or his work with Nicki Minaj, Young Thug, etc.) was the executive producer and the one who approached me to do it. He told me they were going to lose the rights if they didn't get started by a certain date, so I went out of my way to call Aida, my now-wife. She was then just a longtime friend, and I wanted to see if she could get to the meeting and see what she could do on the marketing and publicity side and how we could really get this project going in the right direction. Like she always has, Aida came through and we started full steam ahead.

I was starring as one of the main characters in the movie, Quadir Richards, but I also took on a producer role because Manny was selling me dreams. He was telling me that he was going to get me this amount of money and the film was really going to be my comeback and that I'd really be able to set my life up with that money. Of course, I'm all the way with it at the time!

We wrapped the movie eventually and being that I didn't get paid what I was worth, was no longer on a television show anymore and *that girl* had drained the funds that I had saved, I had no money and therefore, no place to live.

There was still some stuff to wrap up on *True to the Game*, so Manny got me a hotel in Los Angeles down on Wilshire. Now that I had a place to stay, albeit temporary, it got me in a good space to write again and I started working on a new script for a film about the life of the legendary Dock Ellis. Once again, I rang up Aida for help, and as usual, she pulled through.

Aida and I

We were sitting in the hotel talking one day and I just looked at her.

"Man, I don't know why I haven't been with you."

She said the same thing, but of course also made a well-deserved jab about the thots I'd been running through. From that moment on, we were together, and now we're married with a beautiful son.

(As far as the movie, it finally came out in 2017, two

years later. And now Manny and I are planning on making part two and three of the film.)

I'm grateful for the moments that led me to Aida, because I don't think I could have appreciated her in that moment like I did if I hadn't experienced them. As the saying goes, it's always darkest before dawn.

True To The Game

18

THE LONG AND THE SHORT OF IT

M *atthew 4:1-11 reads:*

Then Jesus was led by the Spirit into the wilderness to be tempted by the devil. After fasting forty days and forty nights, he was hungry. The tempter came to him and said, "If you are the Son of God, tell these stones to become bread."

Jesus answered, "It is written: 'Man shall not live on bread alone, but on every word that comes from the mouth of God.'"

Then the devil took him to the holy city and had him stand on the highest point of the temple. "If you are the Son of God," he said, "throw yourself down. For it is written:

"'He will command his angels concerning you, and they will lift you up in their hands, so that you will not strike your foot against a stone.'"

Jesus answered him, "It is also written: 'Do not put the Lord your God to the test.'"

Just Columbus

Again, the devil took him to a very high mountain and showed him all the kingdoms of the world and their splendor. "All this I will give you," he said, "if you will bow down and worship me."

Jesus said to him, "Away from me, Satan! For it is written: 'Worship the Lord your God, and serve him only.'"

Then the devil left him, and angels came and attended him.

Jesus spent 40 days and nights of solitude, prayer and fasting in the wilderness. He knew how dangerous it was to do that from the wild temperatures to the wild animals and the lack of resources, but he still chose to do so to prepare himself for the greater mission – God's mission. Or was he allowing himself to be tempted by Satan?

My temptations for years have come in the form of alcohol, drugs and toxic friendships and relationships. Things that were meant to either end my life or force me to choose a different path, led me to where I am now. I feel like God tests his servants to see if they are fit and I failed the test many times, but I've finally gotten it right. He can see that I'm ready to serve Him, and my life is seeing abundance once again.

Now I'm telling my story in hopes that someone going through something similar can see that there is always hope at the end of the tunnel, no matter how far gone you may feel at times.

I am in the rebuilding process from the ground up, and it's more than just my name in the media that I have to fix. I've burnt so many bridges behind-the-scenes, whether it was my own reckless behavior or some shit that I would get roped into because of someone else – usually *that girl*. Nobody liked my ex-wife. They hated how she spoke to me, because she was always very disrespectful in front of people. She would belittle me a lot in front of anyone no matter who it was, and I didn't even have to say anything — they just knew and didn't like her. So when all the shit really hit the fan with her and I, my peers were reading the headlines just like everybody else, and everyone started really distancing themselves. Nobody came and asked me, they just rolled with it – and my feelings were hurt for a very long time.

I found out later that *that girl* had actually been back-dooring me for a duration of that period as well, telling people that I was abusing her, which is absolutely not true. So when all that came out, it validated her. They initially were rolling with my word, but the headlines seemed to confirm everything she was saying.

I took everything personal for so long, but with growth and rebuilding, I've realized that I was carrying the toxicity around with me too, and everyone really made the right choice in taking a step back. It forced me to take a step back myself and reflect on my own actions as well and slowly but surely, I've been seeing people enter back into my life. It's God's timing.

My Team Xtreme crew (Idris, Zoe and Chris during *The Losers*) were some of the relationships that I really missed the most when I was at my lowest point. It was just such a close-knit group of people that really had each other's back during those three months and even beyond. We would just hang out at one of our houses and we would just be in there chopping it up doing dumb stuff, chilling, Idris would bring his turntables. We only had each other out there and it was just a very special time of bonding. I think Team Xtreme will never be forgotten by any of us, no matter what transpired after. They actually all remained pretty close and still are to this day, and sadly when all of those things went down, nobody knew what to believe about me. It just sucked, because Chris and I were like BEST friends. Even when we came back after the movie, we hung out all the time, but I never mentioned my personal life. And then the headlines hit, and there it went.

About six months ago, Chris got in contact with me to tell me that he missed me, and Aida and I went over to visit him. Man, it felt good to hang out again. He saw that I wasn't drinking and that my wife is amazing, and it all kind of fell together for the good and I just had to let my life shine. That was another thing – it used to be that every other week it was a different chick, but now he could see that I actually did have an understanding of how to pick a good woman.

I've prayed and prayed to the Lord to rebuild my burnt bridges, and people are finally coming back into my life. And honestly, I think they're coming back because they haven't heard anything negative about me in a long time, they see I have a beautiful family – they see I finally fucking got it together to be the man they always knew I could be.

Meagan Good is coming back into my life as well because of films and TV we're doing, and as I've said, she and I used to be tight when we were younger because we grew up near each other. She's another one who believed all that crap when it went down, but our relationship allowed for a dialogue to happen that I believe was needed for both of us to begin to rebuild a friendship.

And then my girl Zoe Saldana, she was the only one who really had my back when everything went down when I got fired from *Scandal*. I had no money for a lawyer because *that girl* took all the money, and Zoe gave me money to get one. I promised her I'd pay her back and every time that I've tried to give her money since, she refuses to take it. She showed up like my sister for real. That's what Team Xtreme was about. You know, you do a lot of movies and you guys are best friends for the duration of the movie but then everybody goes their separate ways, but Team Xtreme — that's not how we went. It was a real friendship and a real bond. It was a sister and brotherhood.

Zoe and Uncle Fish knew the rumors weren't true and that's why they were helping me, and they got disappointed because even after they were helping, there were more headlines of me getting arrested. They were just not seeing me live to my potential.

I want to add that believe it or not, I draw the line at dealing with co-stars in my films. I know this is a random note, but I feel like I've painted quite a picture, and I just want to scale it back at least slightly. The reason that I never have is because when I'm at work, that is my craft.

Even if I have to create chemistry, I'm a master at that. People are so quick to say, "Oh they smashed for sure off camera!" but no, that's not the case. First of all, after the whole Britney thing, I never wanted to mess up the creative for some momentary lustful situation. Secondly, I never want to bring any kind of drama into where my peace is in front of that camera. Thirdly, these actresses – they're a whole other world too. I've always kept it very professional. I've always been close with my co-stars, though.

My first big sis in the game was actually Regina King. We worked together on *This Christmas* in the early stages of my film career, and she always looked out for me on some, "I got you, baby bro!" Then Zoe became another big sister not too long after, and my third was Kate Beckinsale.

Kate and I worked together on *Whiteout* for Warner Bros. in 2007. We were out in Canada filming in Manitoba and Montreal for almost four months, and there wasn't anything to do out there so we really got close. The film was set in Antarctica, so you can just imagine the type of sets we were on all day. I got very close-knit with Kate and her then-husband Len, even after we wrapped and got back to Los Angeles. I'm talking close-knit like I'm Kate's daughter's godfather, or at least I was. We had family vacations and all that. Then I got *Scandal* and Kerry became another big sis too.

I was very close with all of the women I've worked with, and I think that's what took me a long way and is going to continue to be something that moving forward in my career is a positive. Women enjoyed working with me like they enjoyed working with Mark Ruffalo. They feel safe, they know I'm not a pig that would be making passes and making them uncomfortable in the work place or making crass or inappropriate jokes. I make them laugh, we all laugh. A lot! It's always very much about encouraging each other to get the best out of whatever scene we are doing for the greater good of the project. They all are extraordinary thespians something I'm very serious about. So I think that's why I've always gotten exceptionally close to my female co-stars or counterpart, our mutual love and respect of the craft.

It was amazing to have sisters in the game because they looked out for me a lot and wanted me to be everything I was supposed to be and am going to be. I dropped the ball back there in my dealings with my life, and that's another thing looking back I'm like damn, those relationships were so important and valuable to my heart. I love them all from the bottom of my heart. When all that stuff went down, women are going to ride with women and they're going to protect each other, and I have nothing but respect for that. I know that they also wanted to look out for me, but it was just too much.

Zoe and Kate came to me asking what happened

when the headlines started popping up, but Kerry already knew. Zoe was like, "Get out of this thing and get your life back!"

That's the off-camera stuff people don't see – the love and support and this kind of fraternal order. It's a small percent of the world who does what we do as a career. It's pretty special, but people don't see the behind-the-scenes; the camaraderie and the brother and sisterhood in this business. I was truly blessed. The game hated me, especially black actors. I've never been jealous – I think that's one of the most dangerous feelings people can have.

The Champ and I

For a long time, my attitude was, "I've worked with the greatest. Why am I relegated to the shadows?" I wouldn't even read the scripts to the projects I would take on. I'd just be like, "Alright whatever, how much? Alright cool I'll show up." I didn't even read the scripts to these projects I was getting until 15 minutes before rehearsal. I have a family to provide for and my antics forced me to become an acting mercenary. But the rebuild is a great one.

I order my morning smoothie now and it's definitely not a bottle of Chardonnay. I'm working with Mike Tyson and Evander Holyfield doing a series – a show that I actually created, *Heavyweights*. I'm planning on playing Mike myself.

Then Mike has a show that his wife and brother-in-law created (which he's actually starring in) that I'm writing on, so it's really a great way to put my multiple talents to work as my wife simultaneously continues to build her PR company by helping with the project as well. I also have another movie that I've been shooting while developing other films and television projects, so suffice to say, I'm a busy person loading my creative arsenal.

Evander Holyfield, Mike Tyson and I

Some days I get overwhelmed trying to juggle all of these projects that I have my hands in, as well as trying to be the best husband and father that I can be. But in those moments when I find myself being stressed, I remember all that it took to get back to this point. I remember seeing the looming sign to the entrance of the 101 through drunk goggles as I contemplated disappearing from this world. I remember watching *that girl* drive off into the night with a tire that I popped while my daughter sat on her lap. I remember all of the tears that I cried, all of the prayers that I sent up questioning why God can't help me get right. I remember why I'm here.

I've had to fight my entire life — mentally, physically, and spiritually. I've had to fight white boys, Bloods, Crips, my mom, my stepdad, my brothers, the women I've dated...and married...and worst of all, I've had to fight my own demons. I'm done fighting! I don't want to fight anymore.

Us

I'm just grateful to be in place now where I'm not fighting. I'm flowing with the vibrations of the Spirit. I know we're judging by our fruits, and I think my tree is finally starting to bear good fruit and I'm no longer attracting these negative experiences and people. That's a true testament to my wife and the work that I've done on myself. And despite the depths of Hell that I've been through and the journey there and back, I wouldn't change anything for the world because it made me who I am and I love it. I love that I've been through all that because it strengthened me and I'm able to teach, but I'm also able to understand and relate to both sides of the aisle. I understand the white mindset of privilege and sometimes entitlement. I understand the black anger and pain stemming from years of suppression and oppression, and how that's taken a toll on our community. I understand what it is to be a parent and trying to do the best you can. There's no rule book, there's no guide to this thing. I understand what it is to have a lot of money and responsibility. I understand what it is to lose that.

I understand a lot of things that have all been learned through trial and tribulation and that's why I wouldn't change anything for the world. Well maybe just a couple things! My life is ever-growing and changing, and who's to say what the future will deliver? One thing's for sure – the next chapter will be one I can truly be proud of.

To be continued....

My Newest Single

ACKNOWLEDGMENTS

First I would like to thank Kathy Iandoli for creating a safe place for me to begin the writing process. Her help and non judgmental approach was invaluable in the making of this literary time capsule. A big thank you to Marissa Mendez and her collaboration and input into this book. Special thank you to all those who have been a part of my journey. Thanks to the ones who turned their backs because it showed me who was really in my corner. Thank you the ones that reached out a hand to lift me back up. Without that true love and support who knows where I would be. You know who you are! And to my wife, thank you for being there through it all and encouraging me to tell my story.

- Columbus Short

I can't start this off without thanking Kathy Iandoli first and foremost, as this quite literally could not have been possible without you. I LOVE YOU. Thank you for believing in me and giving me the space to be me. Thank you to Columbus for entrusting me with writing your story. I've been a fan since Accepted, dude. This was an honor. Thank you, Carol... I don't know how to say how grateful I am for you without sounding super lame but girl you are truly my soul sister and and I'm so honored to call you my best friend. Thank you to my parents and Farkwad for being as amazing and insane as you all are, because it created me and that's pretty cool so...also you're welcome. Thank you to Victoria, Kiana, Zombz, Melissa, Tunisia and Slim for being there for me every step of the way through everything. I sincerely love you guys. Thank you to Sarah aka Sky Articles for transcribing all of the tapes! That was a HUSTLE and I can't wait to watch you continue to grow and kill it. You're a star. And most importantly, thank you to Marvis for yet another oppor-tunity. Let's get these bags!!!!! This one is dedicated to my mini best friends Jade, Jason and Gia and as always, our angel Parker.

-Marisa Mendez

KINGSTON IMPERIAL

Marvis Johnson — Publisher
Kathy Iandoli — Editorial Director
Joshua Wirth — Designer
Bob Newman — Publicist

Contact:
Kingston Imperial
144 North 7th Street #255
Brooklyn, NY 11249
Email: Info@kingstonimperial.com
www.kingstonimperial.com